GORDON

D1087088

Gordon Brown

Francis Beckett

HAUS BOOKS
London

Copyright © 2007 Francis Beckett

First published in Great Britain in 2007 by Haus Publishing,
26 Cadogan Court, Draycott Avenue, London SW3 3BX
www.hauspublishing.co.uk

The moral rights of the author have been asserted

A CIP catalogue record for this book is available from the British Library

ISBN 978-1-905791-14-9

Typeset in Novarese by MacGuru Ltd
info@macguru.org.uk

Printed and bound by Graphicom in Vicenza, Italy

Cover illustration: Getty Images
Cartoon on the back cover: John Holder

CONDITIONS OF SALE
All rights reserved. No part of this publication may be reproduced, stored in
a retrieval system, or transmitted in any form or by any means, electronic,
mechanical, photocopying, recording or otherwise, without the prior permission
of the publisher.

This book is sold subject to the condition that it shall not, by way of trade
or otherwise, be lent, re-sold, hired out or otherwise circulated without the
publisher's prior consent in any form of binding or cover other than that in which
it is published and without a similar condition including this condition being
imposed on the subsequent purchaser

Contents

Introduction

Maybe it's because, in England, the adjective 'dour' always gets attached to the noun 'Scotsman', that the public perception of Gordon Brown is the opposite of the truth. In private he's an amusing, erudite man with a quiet, musical and attractive dark brown voice, a low, gurgling laugh which you hear often, and almost stately manners.

I wrote this book in three months, finishing at the end of April 2007, and Brown invited me into 11 Downing Street for breakfast just before I finished – for a chat, not for an interview. The difference is that I can't quote what he said, but I can use it to inform what I write, and I have.

We sat in easy chairs at a coffee table, laid for two with cut fruit, croissants and coffee, in a small front room overlooking the garden to the house next door, Number 10. We could see the wisteria tumbling over the lawn, the terrace where in summer many of the Prime Minister's decisions get taken, young Leo Blair's round trampoline surrounded by its cage so that he doesn't hurt himself. It was smaller and more domestic than I expected. I felt a little as I do where I write these words, in my study on the first floor of my suburban home, overlooking my neighbour's brick barbecue, round which in summer we eat kebabs and drink wine.

Brown added to the suburban feel, relaxing as best he could when he knew we had exactly three quarters of an hour before his 9 a.m. cabinet meeting, worrying that I wasn't eating much (I was giving priority to getting some notes down).

I was grateful to him for fitting me into his tight schedule. But of course we could only scratch the surface in the time he could spare. This book, intended to be both a biography and an assessment of Brown's record and of what sort of a Prime Minister Brown is going to be, relies heavily both on published sources and on other interviews.

With my deadline, right from the start, rushing towards me like an oncoming TGV, there was no time to interview everyone to whom I would have liked to talk, or to chase down and reassure those who were fretting about whether or not they ought to talk to me. But I am grateful to those who did talk, without whom this book would have been a poor thing indeed.

Ed Balls, Economic Secretary to the Treasury and Brown's close adviser and confidante since 1984, talked to me helpfully, on the same terms as Brown himself. Wilf Stevenson, Brown's old Edinburgh University friend and director of the Brownite think-tank the Smith Institute, has been a regular source of sensible advice and useful information. Neil Kinnock talked to me at length and with unexpected frankness. I had useful and interesting talks with other political figures: Roy Hattersley, Nick Brown MP, John Edmonds, David Chaytor MP, and a few others who prefer not to be acknowledged, but to whom I am grateful all the same.

The politicians most closely associated with Tony Blair were a lot less forthcoming. Most of those I approached declined to talk to me. Labour politics have a tendency to become tribal. Right now, anyone who writes about politics gets labelled, whether they like it or not, as 'Brownites' or 'Blairites'. There is a remorseless Thatcher-like logic about it: writers are either 'one of us' or they are in the enemy camp.

Perhaps the Blairites identify me as a Brownite. As this book makes clear, and as Brown realised, I have serious criticisms of Brown. But labelling writers tends to be a self-fulfilling prophecy, and the helpfulness of the Brownites and the obstructiveness of the Blairites may be part of the reason (though not the whole reason) why I find myself more sympathetic to Brown than to Blair.

Two previous Brown biographers, William Keegan and Paul Routledge, were generous with their knowledge and insights. So were two old friends in journalism: David Hencke, Westminster correspondent of the *Guardian*, with whom I once wrote a book about Tony Blair; and Martin Bright, political editor of the *New Statesman*. Others who have given me helpful insights include journalists Nigel Jones, Fiona Millar and Harry Conroy; Professor Colin Holmes; and former Brown schoolfellow Liz McVicar. I also benefited from memories and notes of earlier talks, before I began this book, with Nick Kochan, one of the authors of a book about Brown's first year as Chancellor; as well as John Carr, Bob Worcester, Bryan Gould and John Monks, among others.

But breakfast with Brown was still the most useful of the lot. Apart from finding him very good company – which would surprise many people who have not met him, but few people who have – I came away with two overwhelming impressions.

First, he's a historian. I don't simply mean that he has a PhD in history, though he has. I mean that he has a feel for the past. It's not that he was a historian; he still is. He sees the way in which the present follows from the past, and he does not make the mistake of judging what people did in the past by what we know of the present. He sees the 1920s and 1930s as clearly as anyone can see them who did not live through them. He and I could have argued all morning about Maxton and MacDonald, Churchill and Attlee. We have not had a Prime Minister with that sense of history since Harold Macmillan – and Macmillan, for different reasons, is a Prime Minister much in Brown's mind right now, as we shall see.

Second, partly because he was only 16 when he went to university, he is a state school product of the early Sixties, not the late Sixties: of a time before the ersatz revolutionaries of the generation of 1968. He is the product of a time when student radicals were serious-minded, tweed-jacketed, Labour-voting and strongly aware of being the first generation with the chance to go to university even though they had no money, like Neil Kinnock. Though he is only two years older than Tony Blair, he is essentially a man of an earlier generation than Blair; for Blair is the product of a late Sixties public school, looking far more revolutionary but without the grounded radicalism. That, though neither of them realised it for years, is, I think, the unbridgeable gap between them.

1

A Serious Son of the Manse

If the Reverend John Ebenezer Brown had wanted to travel far from his home in Govan, near Glasgow, on 20 February 1951, it would not have been easy. The country was gripped by a rail strike, and the three unions were locked in bad-tempered negotiations with British Rail. That morning's newspapers reported hopes of a breakthrough, but talks broke down during the day. But Revd. Brown was not going anywhere on 20 February. At 8.45 a.m. his wife Elizabeth gave birth to their second son, James Gordon Brown, and Revd. Brown, as always, knew where his duty lay.

While the healthy eight- or nine-pound baby was being born in a nursing home close to his parents' house, the two sides in the rail dispute were taking their case to the Minister of Labour, Aneurin Bevan.

That same morning the Labour Prime Minister, Clement Attlee, and his deputy, Herbert Morrison, spent an hour touring the Festival South Bank site in London, and Morrison, whose baby the building was, told reporters: 'We are going to have this open on the prescribed date. Rumours to the contrary are unfounded.'[1] Morrison was right. The Royal Festival Hall opened when Gordon was three months old.

The rail strike was resolved when he was just four days old. The *Daily Mail* was torn between rejoicing, and splenetic fury because Bevan had given the railwaymen most of what they wanted.

Gordon Brown knows his history. In that sense he will be a Prime Minister in the tradition of Attlee and Macmillan: serious history students who can put their own activities in the context of the past, and who believe that a knowledge of history helps a politician. The other tradition, represented by Tony Blair and Margaret Thatcher, knows little history and sometimes seems to consider history merely a burden to a practical politician, though Blair has said he wishes he had studied history at university instead of law.

The politician who knows his history also knows that the same problems and issues keep recurring, in different forms, for a new generation to deal with. Trade unions and strikes were to preoccupy the Revd. Brown's son for much of his adult life, and he was to be a key (and sceptical) player when Herbert Morrison's grandson, Peter Mandelson, championed another building just a couple of miles east of the Royal Festival Hall, the Millennium Dome, with much less satisfactory results.

Equally, a letter in the *Manchester Guardian* on the day of his birth offers a glimpse of a political world with which Gordon Brown was to become all too familiar:

'Thank you for your footnote to the letter of Mr J.P.W. Mallalieu', wrote the chairman of the Parliamentary Lobby Journalists, Guy Eden. Mallalieu had complained about an article written by the *Manchester Guardian*'s own parliamentary correspondent, and Eden was furious: 'It strikes us as a little strange that Mr Mallalieu, who proclaims himself as an ex lobby correspondent, should have forgotten the rule – accepted by generations of lobby journalists – that nothing overheard in the Palace of Westminster is ever to be published.' The *Manchester Guardian*'s lobby correspondent was 'capable of forming an accurate impression of the proceedings at "private" meetings by methods of which there can be no justifiable complaint'. Non-attributable lobby briefings were to become Tony Blair and Gordon Brown's preferred method of attacking each other.

These were the dying days of Clement Attlee's Labour government. Elected in 1945, its settlement of Britain's internal affairs lasted until the election of Margaret Thatcher in 1979, and its record was the standard against which all Labour governments since, including the ones which contained Gordon Brown, were judged.

It had mounted the first, and still the greatest, assault on the 'five giants' identified by the Beveridge Report during the Second World War: Want, Disease, Ignorance, Squalor and Idleness. Three years before Gordon Brown entered the world, on 5 July 1948, four Acts of Parliament came into effect: the National Insurance Act, the Industrial Injuries Act, the National Assistance Act, and the NHS Act. They were all based on the new principle that, as Attlee put it, 'we must combine together to meet contingencies with which we cannot cope as individual citizens ... They are comprehensive and available to every citizen. They give security to all members of the family.' Or, as Winston Churchill had put it during the war, it meant citizens were looked after 'from the cradle to the grave'. The National Health Service, said Attlee, 'gives a complete cover for health by pooling the nation's resources and paying the bill collectively'. In the 1980s the public-sector trade union NUPE produced a T-shirt proudly worn by then middle-aged men and women with the slogan 'Born in the NHS'. Gordon Brown was a member of the first generation of children to be entitled to wear it, but T-shirts have never been Brown's style.

Britain's war-ravaged economy had to pay the price. There were many voices raised to say that it could not afford to do so; that however worthy the ideas were, they should wait until the finances improved. Could the nation afford it? Would a prudent Chancellor have allowed it? Here is Attlee's answer, given to the House of Commons in 1946:

'The question is asked – can we afford it? Supposing the answer is "No", what does that mean? It really means that the sum total of the goods produced and the services rendered by the people of this country is not sufficient to provide for all our people at all times, in sickness, in health, in youth and in age, the very modest standard of life that is represented by the sums of money set out in the Second

Schedule to this [National Insurance] Bill. I cannot believe that our national productivity is so slow, that our willingness to work is so feeble or that we can submit to the world that the masses of our people must be condemned to penury.'

What he did not say – but what, of course, he knew – is that you cannot have a universal welfare state *and* low taxes. In 1945 the voters knew that too, and elected Labour with their eyes open. It is less clear that they knew that when they elected New Labour in 1997.

By 1951 Attlee's New Jerusalem had lost its shine. His massive majority of 1945 had been reduced to a barely workable one of just five in 1950. Attlee was forced to call another election in October when young Gordon was just eight months old, and although he got more votes than the Conservatives, the Conservatives had an overall majority of 17. The Attlee years were over.

The 1950s was a strait-laced time for a little boy to grow up. Today it is often seen as a glorious Indian summer, before free love and protest came along to ruin things. Tony Blair, born two years after Gordon Brown, sometimes gives the impression that he sees it that way. But the truth is that the relative liberalism of the Thirties had been closed down in the grey post-war years. Britain in the Fifties was a much more repressed and conformist society than it had been before the war.

Anyone younger than Gordon Brown does not know the sort of world where it was illegal to buy *Lady Chatterley's Lover*, to get an abortion, to have a homosexual relationship, or to put on a West End play without first obtaining permission from the Lord Chamberlain. But Gordon Brown knows.

It was a world in which you accepted what your elders, betters and rulers said. In John Osborne's *The Entertainer*, set in 1956, a young man about to go and fight in Suez says: 'Things aren't that bad, and even if they are, there's nothing we can do about it.' The idea that you can change the world, that rebellion and dissent are good, seemed to have been killed off by the hardships of the war and the drab, bleak poverty of the immediate post-war years, not to rise again until the Sixties.

It was a world of convention. 'Short back and sides' a man would say as he walked into the barber, and it would have been unmanly to say anything else. The man, if he was middle class and it was a working day, would have worn a grey suit, baggy trousers with turnups, a white shirt and a tie.

For young Gordon, brought up in the serious-minded home of a Presbyterian Minister, the early years were not a barrel of laughs, but they were secure and comfortable in a home where he knew he was loved. He recalled years later: 'Being brought up as the son of a minister made me aware of community responsibilities that any decent society ought to accept. And strong communities remain the essential bedrock for individual prosperity.'[2] It also made you strongly aware of a vengeful God, before whom you must one day answer for what you have made of your life, as Revd. Brown's sermons made very clear.

When Gordon was three, his parents moved to the other side of Scotland, to Kirkcaldy, where he spent the rest of his childhood. Young Gordon soon embarked on a serious-minded education at Kirkcaldy West Primary School. For schoolchildren, especially clever ones from families like the Browns which valued education, the Fifties represent long hours of boredom, parsing sentences and memorising capital cities. Young Gordon was taught by rote, and he wrote with pencils on slate boards, rubbing out his work with a smelly wet rag, in a very traditional listed school building dating back to 1875.

Kirkcaldy, on the north of the Firth of Forth, is the largest town in Fife, having expanded in the 19th century with the development of the textile, linoleum and coal industries. Its most famous son, before Gordon Brown at any rate, is Adam Smith (1723–90), the political economist and author of *The Wealth of Nations* – and the profit of economic liberalism, the intellectual rock upon which Thatcherism was build. The Adam Smith Institute in London has been the most influential right-wing think-tank of modern times; though one of the historian Gordon Brown's missions, as we shall see, has been to rescue Adam Smith from the right-wing laager into which posterity, in Brown's view unjustly, has imprisoned him.

But in Brown's childhood, Kirkcaldy, as one of his oldest friends Wilf Stevenson points out, was a place with great poverty in it, 'and the church was the one place where people were given opportunity and hope. He saw the poor of the town in the church, and also coming for help afterwards.'

The Revd. John Brown was kind, generous and thoughtful, and not a man to turn the needy from his door. He was an example of decency and rectitude to his three sons. What the church was to Revd. Brown, the Labour Party became to Gordon Brown: the instrument through which they tried to combat poverty. One of Brown's central beliefs is that government can deal with poverty, and has an absolute moral duty to do so. He remembers clearly the misery in the town when the linoleum factory closed with the loss of 550 jobs, the pits closing and thousands of miners being out of work. He was thinking very early: there must be something we can do about unemployment and poverty. His older brother remembers – Brown is too young to remember – how badly the Revd. Brown wanted Labour to win the 1959 general election and do something for the poor; and how disappointed his father was at Harold Macmillan's victory.

Gordon tried to behave as his parents would wish, sometimes with less than perfect results. One day he opened the door to a man who asked for food, and the 10-year-old invited him into the kitchen and sat him down for an impromptu meal. When his parents returned to find him eating at their table, they were less than pleased: the man was the most notorious burglar in the town.

His father's approval mattered terribly to young Gordon, and we can see throughout his childhood his striving to earn it. It remained important to him throughout his life. When he produced his first budget as Chancellor of the Exchequer in 1997, he received plaudits from all over the world, but the discovery of his father's words, quoted in a local newspaper, seem to have given him more pleasure than any of them. You can hear in the phrases the stern, measured tones of the elderly minister: 'He spoke very wisely and quite humbly. I don't think there was any sort of show about him or anything like that. I don't think he had any jokes at all, as far as I can remember. It was a good speech, well put together.'[3]

His mother was a remarkable woman too – less of an influence than his father, but someone he admired. During the Second World War, she had worked in London, decoding intelligence, but she did not like to talk about it much. She was a quiet but forceful and intelligent woman.

Young Gordon was dreadfully precocious. He recited 'Thomas the Tank Engine' stories by heart in their entirety at the age of four, and constantly demanded harder work from his primary school teachers. So he was fast-tracked a year early to Kirkcaldy High School – still following in the footsteps of Adam Smith, whose early education was at the same school. But the old building in which Adam Smith learned was no longer adequate after the Second World War. A new one, light, airy, modern and designed to cope with the new customers created by the 1944 Education Act, had been opened in 1958, shortly before Brown went there.

The school, says a fellow pupil – Elizabeth (Betty) Dingwall, now Liz McVicar – was 'a good academic high school with strict teaching, and would have been the model for Gordon of what a good education should be. It got good results and took a lot of working class kids and made them the first generation of their families to go to university.' There were very few middle-class families, she says – the son of the Manse would have been about as classy as it got, and much more so than most pupils. 'Doctors, dons, people like that who had any money, their children went by train to Edinburgh to go to school.'

With Brown at Kirkcaldy High School was one of his earliest friends from primary school, Murray Elder, who was to become a lifelong political friend and colleague. These two brainy boys were part of an educational experiment by which the *crème de la crème* – the cleverest of those who were clever enough to go to grammar school, judged on the old method of IQ – were fast-tracked a year early, and at the age of 10 were put into a special intensively-taught class of 11 boys and 25 girls. And as if that wasn't enough shame for one small boy, his father was the school chaplain.

He thought it was all a very bad idea. In May 1967, he typed out an essay saying exactly what he thought of it.

'I watched as each year one or two of my friends would fail under the strain. I saw one girl who every now and then would disappear for a while with a nervous breakdown. I stood by as a friend of mine, who I knew was intelligent enough, left school in despair after five years of strain with no university or higher qualifications. I thought continually of how it could have been for these young guinea pigs, how the strain of work, the ignominy and rejection of failure could have been avoided. All this, I thought I saw better than any educationalist in his ivory tower.'[4]

It's a remarkable analysis for a 15-year-old boy, and the experience influenced his view on education. He still thinks they were pushed too hard. Today his friends are sure that he opposes selection (though he is cautious about committing himself) as well as the 11-plus system still in operation in parts of England, and supports the non-selective comprehensive education introduced by the Wilson government, and later rejected by the Blair government. Whether he is likely to do anything about it as Prime Minister, no one knows for certain, but campaigners for a return to the idea of comprehensive education have been muttering 'wait for Gordon' to each other for years.

Brown was in the first year group ever to be subject to this experiment, and in his year the children were chosen solely on IQ tests. In the second year, other criteria were added, and one of the children chosen was Elizabeth Dingwall. Today she is an educational psychologist, and she says it made the children 'an outgroup in the school' and thinks it convinced Brown of the harm done by selection at the age of 11. 'Adolescence is hard enough without the whole year knowing you are supposed to be cleverer', she says.

It meant that he took his O-levels two years early, at 14, and his Highers – the Scottish equivalent of A-levels – at 15, getting five straight As. This was an extraordinary achievement, marking him out very early as one of the brightest and brainiest of his generation. And it was not even achieved at the expense of being a boring little swot. Gordon Brown's sports master described him as 'a super all-round athlete'[5] – a first-class runner, footballer and rugby player. Nor was he just a beefy swot. He was a star of the literary and debating societies, played the violin in the school orchestra, and jointly edited the school magazine. And yes, since you ask, he was a social success too, gregarious, witty, and attractive to girls. He was clearly an insufferable 15-year-old.

That's what 15-year-old Betty Dingwall thought, anyway. When a message was brought to her across the playground that Gordon Brown wanted to take her out, she sent back a firm 'no'. For although Brown may have been a social success in his own part of the school, there was another part which rather despised his conventional, clean-living, rugby-playing, hard-working set. 'To us hippies he was another fumbling adolescent' she says. 'We saw him as a very straight son of the Manse.' *went to grammar school*

Right then, just a very few miles away, at the Scottish public school of Fettes, 13-year-old Tony Blair was beginning his chequered school career. He was miserable, but by the time he, too, reached the age of 15 he had found out how to work the system and make himself as comfortable as could be in an old-fashioned English-style public school. He did not shine academically, had little to do with school societies (except for drama), refused to play rugby, and teased the masters unmercifully. But he was very attractive to girls.

Geographically close they may have been, but the two boys were as unlikely to meet as if they lived on Mars and Venus. Blair, like most Fettes boys, mixed mostly with other wealthy upper-class children from other Scottish public schools. He would almost certainly not have heard of Kirkcaldy High School, a place on another planet – and, Fettes boys would have assumed, a vastly inferior planet. Blair was two generations away from poverty. Brown lived among people like Blair's poor Scottish grandparents, and went to school with children who remembered what life was like for the poor before the National Health Service. 'Their elders spoke of the poor abandoning treatment in hospitals when their money was spent, and asking doctors about the cost of the visits and medicine before deciding whether their finances were adequate for them to receive treatment.'[6]

In the summer of 1967, aged 16, Gordon Brown left Kirkcaldy High School and started at once as a student at Edinburgh University, which his older brother John already attended, and where his younger brother Andrew was soon to follow him. It was the high point of radical student rebellion. Harold Wilson had been Labour Prime Minister for three years, and was condemned on campuses all over Britain for being insufficiently radical. In Edinburgh that summer, during the Edinburgh Festival, Brown could, if he chose, have toured the fringe and found some of the most radical youthful drama to be seen anywhere. But vague radical politics, and angry unconstructive drama, were not the sort of idle intellectual pursuits that attracted the Revd. Brown's witty and gregarious, but clever and serious-minded, son.

2

The Reluctant Student Politician

Within days of Brown's arrival at Edinburgh University in the autumn of 1967, a personal disaster hit him, which had a profound effect on both his character and his thinking. He found out that he was soon to lose the sight in his left eye – and was in danger of losing the sight in his right eye as well. He faced the real possibility of going completely blind at 16.

During a rugby match six months earlier, he had emerged from a scrum with impaired vision, which he ignored in the hope that the problem would go away. It didn't. A few weeks later he headed a ball during a football match and the vision worsened. Detached retinas in both eyes had become more severe in the weeks that he had tried to ignore the problem. After his operation he had to lie absolutely still in a darkened hospital ward, for six months, terrified every moment that he was to be completely blind for the rest of his life; and he missed the whole of his first term at university.

His right eye was saved. Contact sports like rugby and football, which he had enjoyed so much and shown so much talent for, were banned for the rest of his life, and the terror and misery of those six months have never quite gone away. Friends say that it damaged his confidence permanently, and that Brown thinks it makes a greater difference to his appearance than it actually does make. A journalist who knows him well believes it left him terrified of blindness and obsessed by death.

Years later, on holiday in Cape Cod in 1997, Brown recalled how 'he lost his eye in a rugby match when somebody scraped their boot across his face … he was required to lie horizontal and virtually stationery for a matter of months, as the doctors believed that if the eye and the retina remained completely still they would bond back. For that period he was registered blind, and he appeared to shudder just thinking of it. In fact, within a matter of weeks, the cells bonding the retina on his left eye died, and he lost its use.'[1]

But he could see out of one eye, he could read, he could work, and he still had his brilliant mind and attractive personality. Life, when he made a belated start on his studies in Edinburgh in April 1968, was good.

Gordon Brown and Tony Blair, though neither had heard of the other, were now very close to each other. Just a couple of miles separate the portentous old pile that is Fettes from the centre of Edinburgh, where Brown lodged. Blair, just starting on his A-levels, frequented the student pubs, dodging Fettes masters. It's perfectly possible that they might have been in the same pub at the same time, and a startling contrast they would have made: 15-year-old Blair and a couple of like-minded friends, raucous, wealthy, anglicised, apolitical, public school ersatz rebels, full of what they thought was the spirit of the Sixties; 17-year-old Brown, with drinking companions a year or two older than himself, tweed-jacketed, serious-minded, left-wing, clever, a Scottish lad o'pairts, obviously a young man with gravitas and a future. Only two years separate them, but they are men of two different generations, with two different approaches to the world and how it should be re-ordered.

Brown was very quickly a figure in student politics. His was not the fashionable late-Sixties student politics of unfocused radicalism, but the sober and serious-minded radicalism of the late Fifties and early Sixties generation of students, the first undergraduate generation to which working-class families were significant contributors. He had more in common with that earlier generation, like Neil Kinnock at Cardiff University in the early Sixties – Labour voters all, young men (and occasionally women) who owed their chance in life to the Attlee settlement and knew it – than with the generation of 1968 and revolution. He was much more likely to wear the Cardiff student president Neil Kinnock's white shirt, college tie and V-necked jumper, than the shoulder-length hair and late Sixties finery later sported by Tony Blair.

Edinburgh is an ancient university with a proud academic tradition, whose earlier alumni included James Boswell, Charles Darwin and David Hume. In 1967 it was often a preferred choice for the clever young Scot who, had he been an Englishman, might have wanted to go to Oxbridge. It was just starting to be seen as a second-best for English students who did not quite make Oxbridge, but to Scots like Brown it was the university of choice. And Brown was its youngest post-war student, with a scholarship as well.

Not only that, he was an immediate success, socially as well as academically. Henry Drucker, an American who had recently arrived to teach politics at the university, calls him 'an important figure, even as an undergraduate. He was hugely popular, a natural politician: totally self-assured'.[2] But, just as he had done at school, he managed the difficult trick of combining social success with academic success, becoming known as 'Beaver Brown' for his hard work.

He lived in untidiness bordering on squalor, first in a small flat in the Grassmarket, just behind Edinburgh Castle, and then in a shared house at 48 Marchmont Road, where in time he gave what came to be considered some of Edinburgh's best student parties. He grew his black hair long (but not very long), wrote for the student newspaper (to which he was introduced by his brother John, already a figure at the university), actively promoted the Rag Week (known in Edinburgh simply as 'Charities'), and joined the Labour Party in 1969 (but prudently declined to join the Campaign for Nuclear Disarmament).

It was the time of student radicalism, of sit-ins all over the country – over Vietnam, over South Africa, and over the sometimes petty restrictions universities imposed on the lives of their students.

Gordon Brown may not have been a typical Sixties product, but he shared his generation's misguided contempt for Harold Wilson. The pollster Peter Kelner spoke for many of us who were young and political in the late Sixties and early Seventies when he said that he wanted to offer an apology to the ghost of Harold Wilson. We attacked him for betrayal, for example because of his failure to condemn American aggression in Vietnam. But he kept us out of Vietnam, despite pleas and threats from President Lyndon Johnson, when most other Prime Ministers would have been convinced by the immediate needs of the Atlantic alliance, and the threat of America's power to cripple Britain's economy. The Wilson government's often decried economic record is not bad at all either, seen in retrospect, and Wilson made such cautious moves towards greater equality as the difficult economic circumstances allowed.

But Gordon Brown's generation wanted real change, and wanted it now. At 12 he learned to despise the new Prime Minister Sir Alec Douglas-Home, who had to fight a by-election in Kinross and West Perthshire in order to move to the House of Commons. On a family holiday, he followed Douglas-Home from meeting to meeting (and this was Brown's holiday – even at 12 Gordon Brown was serious and political) and was 'amazed and appalled' that the candidate made the same speech wherever he went. He loved the new satirical television programme *That Was the Week That Was* which started when he was 11 and taught a whole generation not to have exaggerated respect for top politicians. And in 1971 the 20-year-old final-year undergraduate, in an article in the student newspaper, wrote of the student politicians' 'promises and pledges – words so devalued by Harold Wilson'.

After his visit to the work-in at Upper Clyde Shipbuilders in 1971 he wrote in the student newspaper: 'Whatever happens, the Clyde workers will have made the point that the right to work forged in Beveridge's time must he restated in Wilson's super-efficient managerial society ...'[3] The words 'super-efficient managerial society' appeared in a couple of

Brown's articles about this time, always referring to Wilson, and you can hear the sneer in them. None of these views – about Wilson, about managerialism, about Vietnam – would be likely to appeal to the 'Iron Chancellor' today.

Edinburgh was prudent by national standards, and Gordon Brown was prudent by Edinburgh standards. He was not among the 100 or so students who occupied the campus appointments office, though he agreed with their cause. They were protesting about the arrival at the university of recruiters from Barclays Bank, which was accused of investing heavily in white-ruled Rhodesia. Ian Smith had made his unilateral declaration of independence – UDI – in 1965. Brown's line, says Professor Drucker, was 'that a sit-in only worked when the students had already won'.

So it is an odd irony that Gordon Brown became, almost by accident, a standard-bearer for student power, a national icon for the student radicals of the Sixties and early Seventies. By the time he was finished with Edinburgh University, his name was nationally known, even though he hardly left Edinburgh and took little part in the work of the National Union of Students, which at about that time was absorbing so much of the energy of his future cabinet colleagues Charles Clarke (NUS president 1975–7) and Jack Straw (NUS president 1969–71.)

When a chance came his way to make a real difference – and a name for himself in the process – he grabbed it with both hands. The university invested deeply in the apartheid state of South Africa, but kept it secret. In 1970 a copy of the stockbroker's report which proved the extent of this investment was left in a toilet, and an anonymous call was made to the student newspaper, *Student*, to alert them to its presence. Brown was part of the small team, under publications board chairman Jonathan Wills, which produced a four page *Student Special* with the story.

The next year, having taken Wills's place as chairman of the publications board and also become chairman of the Labour Club, he proposed a motion at the Students' Representative Council (SRC) that the students should take the old-established and essentially honorific post of Rector of the University, and turn it into a real power in the hands of students, which would counter the power of the university itself.

Past Rectors, elected by all members of the university, had been chosen from the great and the good. The first rector, when the post was established in 1859, was the Chancellor of the Exchequer and future Prime Minister, W E Gladstone, and famous politicians, actors and various other celebrities had held the post ever since. Now Brown wanted the SRC to accept in principle that it would be a good idea for the next Rector to be a student at the university – and to have real power, taking the chair at the University's Court. A student had stood for the post in 1968 and lost, but Brown was determined that this time the ground was to be properly prepared. Once he had got this motion through the SRC, he started to campaign for his candidate, his predecessor as chairman of the publications board, Jonathan Wills. The establishment candidate was the satirist Willie Rushton.

Brown's man won a spectacular victory. It looked like marking a real turning point in the university's history, and the principal, Sir Michael Swann, was furious. But Jonathan Wills did not want to serve out his three-year term, and left the post after one year, in 1972. It seems that Wills wanted to return to his beloved Shetland, for he was a much less driven character than Brown, his main interest in life being birdwatching and boating around the shores of Shetland, where he has spent most of his life, also working there as a journalist.

That year Gordon Brown graduated with a First in history, and he was about to start on a PhD. He had given a lot of thought to power: how it was obtained, how it was used. He had acquired a taste for the politics of work, visiting the work-in at Upper Clyde Shipbuilders. But Wills's decision left him in pole position, the student with the best chance of winning the job.

This time the establishment candidate was Sir Fred Catherwood, head of the construction group Laing and a former director general of the National Economic Development Council. Brown's campaign foreshadowed the glitz of future New Labour campaigns: mini-skirted girls called Brown's Sugars wore T-shirts saying 'Gordon for me'. He discovered that Catherwood had an undeclared interest: Laing was involved in building work for the university. The principal, Sir Michael Swann, predicted that after Wills the students would want 'a more traditional type of rector' but he was wrong. Brown won by 2,264 votes to Catherwood's 1,308.

Brown, like most members of the New Labour cabinet, went to university at a time when students paid no tuition fees, and were entitled to a means-tested grant for living expenses. So, like every student activist in the country, he was quickly enlisted to campaign for the National Union of Students' grants claim. The grant was £455 a year, and the NUS claim was for £510. Brown's approach was studiously careful and moderate. The NUS won a little more money from the government, though nothing like as much as they wanted.

Brown was a busy and active Rector. He prevented the Court from instituting admission charges to see an art collection, and failed to force the withdrawal of South Africa and Rhodesia from the 1973 Commonwealth Universities Conference in Edinburgh. But it was his activity on internal university matters that led the university establishment to dislike him so thoroughly. Brown wanted greater powers for the Rector, and a principal to replace Swann who was elected directly by the staff and students. He also wanted to democratise the composition of the Court, proposing to fill two vacancies with the secretary of Craigmillar tenants' group and the president of Edinburgh Trades Council (the local branch of the Trades Unions Congress).

They gave him none of these things, but they did get very sick of him, and in April 1973 the Court moved against him, proposing a rule change to end the Rector's right to chair Court meetings, and voting to exclude Brown's assessor, a former student president who spoke to the Court for the students, on the grounds that he had once led an occupation of his college.

Brown took the Court to court, and won. The Court wanted to take their case to the Privy Council, but they learned that their Chancellor, the Duke of Edinburgh, backed Brown, and without his support, they could not hope for much in that quarter. It was game, set and match to the Rector. How had Brown got at the Duke? The answer was a surprising one, considering that he was apparently the voice of the People against the Establishment. His girlfriend at the time, fellow student Princess Margarita, daughter of the exiled King of Romania, had a word with her godfather, the Duke of Edinburgh. Sir Michael, who loathed all student rectors, but Brown especially because he was effective, left in September 1973 to become chairman of the BBC governors.

Brown ended his term of office in summer 1975. At first sight it seems that he had made a real, lasting change. In fact, after Brown's three-year term, the university has never again elected a student rector. And this is no accident: Brown did a deal. He agreed that in future students could not stand for Rector. He traded it for a student seat on the Court, as of right. So Brown was succeeded by the establishment candidate, the host of television's *Mastermind*, Magnus Magnusson.

But something of the spirit that Wills and Brown created has lived on. Last year (2006) the university elected a young Green Party Member of the Scottish Parliament, Mark Ballard, a lifelong environmental campaigner, as Rector. Mr Ballard graduated from Edinburgh University in 1994. He was born in 1971, the year that Jonathan Wills became the first student rector. Perhaps that is Brown's legacy to Edinburgh University: a Court with a student sitting on it, and a more serious attitude to the job of Rector, a desire to make a statement when electing one – for the statement made by the election of Mr Ballard is unmistakeable.

The University undoubtedly gained from Brown's rectorship, but did Brown? He seems not to have thought so. On the face of it, this is surprising. He was just 22, and had been a key mover and shaker in the university and a nationally known figure. He had taken on the establishment and won. Most people of his age would look back on what he had done with a kind of wistful wonder. But Gordon Brown already had his eyes firmly fixed on the horizon. He wished he had done something less glamorous, which would have provided a more solid foundation for the political career he already knew he was determined to have. 'I feel in retrospect I could have done more if I had stood for the local council instead of being Rector. It became a bit of a diversion', he told Paul Routledge.

He learned a lot about politics in the real world, and about how to get what you want, and he made a reputation as a young politician with inspiration and bravado. But he also made powerful local enemies who ensured that he did not get what he wanted next, a full-time university lectureship while he finished his PhD thesis.

Their dislike was to follow him around for a while. There's a strange archive in the university library, and for some reason available on the internet, which breathes fury and resentment. While the letters are reproduced, all the important names have been blacked out, even when they are well known or obvious – for example, the name of the returning officer who certified that Brown had won the Rectorship, and even the name of the candidate he beat.

Some of it is hilariously funny as an illustration of the fury and resentment Brown caused the university authorities, and their trivial means of obtaining revenge. Here's the assistant secretary of the university writing to the secretary – at great length, but I will only quote the beginning, complete with censored names:

'**** of the Rector's office was referred to me in ****'s absence to advise on her request to **** of our Xerox copying section, on whether he could provide a free Xerox copy of a document of some 60–100 pages which appeared to be a paper on higher education. **** did not know who the author was. She believed it was a paper prepared by someone other than the Rector, which the Rector wished to have a copy of … I suggested that, apart from any other considerations, the University had to be particularly careful about possible breaches of copyright where use of the Xerox machine is concerned …' Brown was left in no doubt how a bureaucracy behaves when forced to accommodate an interloper.

The resentment did not die away until long after he had left the job. In 1975, two years after he had ceased to be Rector, they were still writing cross letters about the report he had written. 'I would of course point out,' writes ****, the Secretary of the University, to ****, the librarian at Liverpool University's Institute of Extension Studies, in November 1976, 'that this report is the result of an unofficial action taken by the previous Rector of the University, Mr Gordon Brown, and is in no way an official report of the University of Edinburgh.'[4]

The many, many furious letters and memoranda in this ludicrous collection give a pretty clear idea of how the university regarded Brown. They were prepared to put pretty well any obstacle that came to hand in the way of his doing anything he wanted to do, however harmless or trivial. After his term as Rector ended, he would have liked a university lectureship at Edinburgh, but the university would not give him one, though his qualifications for it were good. They let him teach part time for a while. They were really, really sick of him. He had made them look foolish and small-minded, and they reacted foolishly and small-mindedly.

Years later, when he was Shadow Chancellor, he received a handsome apology and an honorary degree from the then Vice Chancellor, Stuart Sutherland, and he felt that closed the account. Many of us would be proud to have done all that he did as Rector, and to have made such powerful enemies at so young an age, but it is not an episode on which Brown likes to dwell.

If Brown were a natural rebel, never happier than when pricking the pomposity of the powerful, these letters would be treasured mementoes of a glorious three years. But Brown is nothing of the kind. He is, and always has been, serious and political, and regretted making powerful enemies in Edinburgh's political establishment. Still, the experience no doubt came in handy years later when he had to make civil servants do what he wanted.

Nor had he done himself unalloyed good with the young men who in years to come were to be his political colleagues. Charles Clarke was President of the National Union of Students in Brown's last year as rector, and found him a little haughty – Clarke was used to NUS politics, which were rougher, rowdier and ruder than Brown was used to in comparatively genteel Edinburgh. Nonetheless, they uneasily yoked themselves together to demand higher student grants, and nothing more was heard from either of them on the subject for 30 years until, as Chancellor and Education Secretary, they imposed tuition fees on Britain's now grantless students. But the dislike between them resurfaced, as we shall see.

3

The Greasy Pole of Scottish Labour Politics

Gordon Brown never saw student politics as an activity for a serious man. He could not have done what Charles Clarke did, and go into student politics consciously aiming for the top. He had become Rector because he was the obvious student candidate. In a sense, the Rectorship had almost dropped into his lap. But he was bored with constant, grinding battles against a hostile bureaucracy. Brown does not mind battles, but he likes to survey what is at stake first, and make sure it is worth the bloodshed required to get it – a trait which is often wrongly portrayed as weakness.

Academic politics, it's said, are as fierce and bitter as they are because so little is at stake. Brown was pretty sure that the small victories obtainable on campus were not worth it. So by the time his term of office as Rector came to an end in 1975, he had already moved on. He knew all the power brokers in the Labour Party in Scotland, he knew where the levers of power were located and what it took to make them move, and he had been a foot soldier in a general election campaign. He had made a start on his PhD thesis about the Labour Party in Scotland, 1918–29. He cultivated his political contacts assiduously.

He had watched from the Rector's office the demise of the Conservative government under Edward Heath. Heath was, and remains, the only Prime Minister since 1945 to have put an alliance with Europe before an alliance with the USA. His unexpected election victory in

1970 allowed him to achieve the goal of a lifetime, and bring Britain into what was then called the Common Market; but the economic and political circumstances of the time did not allow him to do much else. Rocketing oil prices, fuelled partly by the Yom Kippur War in 1973, and the growing strength and militancy of Britain's trade unions combined to create a political straitjacket.

Nothing more clearly illustrates how far we have travelled in three decades. In 1974 trade unions were a real power in the land, and their role as a part of the state was accepted by governments of all persuasions. Heath, a one-nation Tory of the sort that had been dominant since the war, saw them as the legitimate voice of working people. His government had spent three years unsure whether to confront the trade unions or reach an accommodation with them. He and Jack Jones, the powerful leader of the Transport and General Workers Union (and probably the second most powerful union leader Britain ever knew, after Ernest Bevin) liked and respected each other – Jones preferred Heath to Labour leader Harold Wilson.

But Heath stumbled into a confrontation with the miners' union, with its formidable industrial strength and charismatic leadership. Scots were prominent in its leadership, and Brown, who knew where power in Scottish Labour politics resided, had made sure he got to know men like Mick McGahey, a Communist who smoked and drank whisky all day, had a voice that sounded as though he gargled with granite, and was one of the most respected leaders and most strategic thinkers the unions ever threw up. Another Scot, Laurence Daly, was the miners' general secretary, who stomped the country in 1974 telling everyone that, in the wake of the Lord Lambton scandal, the government ought to pay the miners what they wanted, since cabinet ministers were prepared to pay more than that to 'ladies of easy virtue, for what I understand is considerably less than an eight hour shift'. The historian in Brown must have treasured their friendship, for Daly and McGahey embodied the proud history of the mineworkers' union.

By February 1974 the miners had almost brought the Heath government to its knees. Power shortages had forced Heath to declare a three-day week. Heath then called an election on the question 'Who governs?'. If he won, he had a mandate to face out and defeat the miners. If he lost – though no one put it exactly like this – Labour would settle with the miners, more or less on the miners' terms.

When the election was called, Brown swiftly made himself available as a foot-soldier for the Labour candidate for Edinburgh Central, Robin Cook. Cook, six years older than Brown, was another clever, political young Scot with a degree from Edinburgh University. He worked, as the young Neil Kinnock had done, as a tutor for the Workers Educational Association (WEA), and he was a member of Edinburgh Council. These two facts were almost a way of shouting to the world: 'I want to be a Labour MP!'

Cook's father was a headmaster, and his grandfather had been a miner blacklisted for helping to organise the 1926 General Strike. Brown had met Cook at University, but they only overlapped briefly – Cook's last year was Brown's first. Now, in February 1974, Brown put his heart and soul into securing Cook's election for the marginal seat, recruiting his friends to knock on the doors of working-class areas. At least one of Brown's biographers thinks that the seeds of resentment between the two were sewn during the election. He thought Cook standoffish. 'Too often [Cook] had drunk whisky alone at one end of the Abbotsford's bar while [Brown and his friends] had drunk beer at the other.'[1]

Cook won Edinburgh Central, and Wilson won the election, but by the narrowest of margins and without an overall majority. Brown was invited to the miners' welfare club in Edinburgh to be toasted by Mick McGahey – an extraordinary honour in labour movement circles in 1974. Harold Wilson returned to Downing Street and called a second election in October the same year, which gave him an overall majority of just four seats. This time Brown might have been a candidate for himself, for the (at that time) probably un-winnable seat of Edinburgh South, at the age of just 23, but narrowly lost the nomination.

At the same time he was building his reputation with the publication of two collections of essays by prominent left-wing Scottish thinkers. First came the *Red Paper on Education*, in 1970. The title made it clear that this was the young radical's answer to the Black Papers on education coming out at that time from a group of right-wing educationalists. Then in 1975, his last year as Rector, Brown recycled the title to produce *The Red Paper on Scotland*, a much more ambitious project designed as a radical manifesto for the future of Scotland. It was published by the Edinburgh University Publications Board, which had been the launch-pad for Brown's Rectorship campaign.

The debate on devolution so far, wrote Brown, had 'engendered a barren, myopic, almost suffocating consensus which has tended to ignore Scotland's real problems – our unstable economy and unacceptable level of unemployment, chronic inequalities of wealth and power and inadequate social services'. Brown planted himself firmly on the pro-devolution side at a time when the Scottish Labour Party was still divided on the question.

Brown's introduction to the *Red Paper on Scotland* was as radical as the young man who produced it, and as radical as mainstream politics were in the early Seventies, before Margaret Thatcher arrived and shifted the agenda. It was, wrote Brown, 'increasingly impossible to manage the economy both for private profit and the needs of society as a whole'. Successive Labour governments had failed by not being socialist enough. Socialism used to be a moral imperative, but had degenerated into 'little more than a scheme for compensating the least fortunate in an unequal society'. He called for 'a massive and irreversible shift of power to working people, a framework of free universal welfare services controlled by the people who use them'. He wanted all essential industries nationalised, under workers' control and without compensation, a view which was radical in 1974 and would be revolutionary today. The nation has travelled a very long way in three decades, and Gordon Brown has travelled with it. Yet the fact that he once believed these things endears him to Labour people of his generation, even though he no longer believes them.

The fact that Tony Blair never believed them is part of what gives Blair the aura of a cuckoo in Labour's nest. It is the long-abandoned beliefs of a young radical that will ensure Gordon Brown an initial welcome as Labour's leader from his party. He is no longer, in the traditional sense of the word, a socialist. But he was once. He's thought about it. He speaks the language. He's felt what they feel. He's family.

After 1975, no longer Rector and clear that his future was politics, Brown needed a job. Robin Cook, like Neil Kinnock a few years earlier, had chosen the WEA as his staging post between university and parliament. This would probably not have suited the fiercely serious Brown, a man who is constantly, restlessly, learning new things.

A full-time lectureship at Edinburgh was ruled out – the university establishment could not wait to see the last of him – but Glasgow College of Technology offered him a lectureship in politics, and for four years he commuted to Glasgow from his flat in Marchmont Road. The job left him plenty of time to do all the things an aspiring Labour politician needed to do: become chairman of his branch, then secretary of his constituency party, and keep his eyes peeled for a parliamentary seat, which came up quite fast, in 1976. He got the nomination for Edinburgh South, which might be winnable in a good year.

Paul Routledge interviewed friends to uncover the Brown of this period: 'A prodigious worker, attending meetings three nights a week and devoting all his weekends to political activity ... He carried around plastic bags stuffed with newspaper cuttings and statistical papers on issues close to his heart.' The plastic bags remained a part of his persona for years, until they were eventually replaced by official Treasury boxes.

But there was a personal life there too, and it was sometimes a dark one. In 1974 he had to have another operation on his good eye, and once again faced the danger that he might emerge completely blind. His eye was saved by pioneering surgery done by Edinburgh-based Asian eye surgeon Dr Hector Chowla, who was able to hold it together with what Brown calls 'a form of sellotape'. The memory, and the terror of blindness, still makes him shiver. His sight is very poor – at the despatch box he has to have a pile of books to rest his notes on, and the notes have to be in large writing. He knows that his good eye will deteriorate with age. He can see and he can read, but the time will come when he cannot.

And as politics absorbed all his time, his relationship with Margarita – his Romanian princess from student days – came under growing strain. They were in love – all their friends were clear about that – and they had fun together, but she felt ignored and taken for granted, no doubt because she was. Planned visits to parties or to the cinema always seemed to be getting cancelled as the telephone summoned her lover to yet another vital political meeting at the last moment. To the really dedicated politician on the rise, all meetings are vital. You can't afford to let anything happen behind your back. The first rule is: be there.

Margarita wanted to try to make the relationship work, and to know if it had a long term future. Brown wanted to know that, too, but when she arranged a weekend in a country cottage and had the telephone cut off, Brown was furious. The fact that she did not share his political views worried him – she was not much interested in politics, and picked up her views largely from the minor royalty she mixed with before she met him. She worried that politics always came first with him. Eventually, one of them broke off the relationship – it is not clear who. But it is clear that neither of them ever quite got over it.

Soon after he secured the Edinburgh South nomination came the sniff of a better opportunity. Hamilton was a Labour seat, and its MP died unexpectedly just after Brown secured the Edinburgh South nomination. Some local activists liked the idea of putting up a young man with colossal energy, brains, charm and commitment. It would have meant a spectacular start to a parliamentary career, entering Parliament at 25, and at a by-election, an event which is always high-profile and often turns a politician into a national figure overnight.

But he decided not to try and get it. He rather implied that he was doing so out of loyalty to Edinburgh South. This piece of quixotic gallantry was at best only a small part of the reason. There were two other factors. One – and according to his friends the key factor – was that, that same year, Brown's parents moved to Hamilton, where his father was now the local minister. They – especially his mother – would not have liked the inevitable media intrusion in their lives at all with their son standing for election to become the local MP.

The second was the stark political reality that he might well not win the nomination, and would make enemies trying. In those days big trade unions still largely controlled the Labour parliamentary nomination in some seats, and Hamilton was General and Municipal Workers Union (GMWU) territory. Its candidate, GMWU official George Robertson, won the nomination and the seat. He would probably have done so even if Brown's hat had been in the ring, though powerful people were advising Brown that if he made a real fight of it, he could probably win. Brown probably thought that the damage the battle would do, both to the Labour Party in Hamilton and to him personally, was not worth it for the chance of victory.

There is a strange foretaste here of Brown's 1994 decision not to stand against Blair for the Labour leadership. The same political calculation was made, and on both occasions his decision was interpreted by his enemies, and some of his friends, as a fatal weakness and lack of ruthlessness.

There was one more chance to hasten his entry into Parliament. He was sounded out to be candidate for Leith, which was much better Labour territory than Edinburgh South. He did not go for it. The pattern repeats itself. Brown's friends say he felt obligated in honour to Edinburgh South. His enemies, represented most coherently in this case by Tom Bower, say it was a dreadful career mistake prompted by the indecision and insecurity which has always made him second best to Tony Blair.

Still, he was not doing badly. A successful speech at the Scottish Labour Party conference in Troon in 1976 was followed by election to Labour's Scottish Executive in 1977. His dramatic appearance, radical oratory and serious, gravelly voice made him something like a spokesman for the Seventies generation in Scotland.

But he knew that, while his own political career was prospering, his party was in poor shape. These were the downhill years for Labour, the troubled prelude to a generation of Thatcherism. The bubble of union power was bound to burst sometime soon, for unions seemed very powerful, but did not really have the power with which they were credited by both their friends and their enemies. All the seeds of the divisions of the Eighties were present by the mid-Seventies.

James Callaghan succeeded Harold Wilson as Prime Minister in 1976, the year that Gordon Brown went to lecture at Glasgow College of Technology. Callaghan inherited a government which once had an overall majority of four, and now had no overall majority at all, being kept in power by the Liberals.

Two years later Callaghan made what many, both at the time and in retrospect, thought was the worst error of judgement of his career. As the TUC conference that autumn, it had been widely trailed – and never denied – that Callaghan was going to use his speech to announce an immediate general election. Union leaders, welcoming him to the platform, shared the general expectation, and the GMWU leader David Basnett was already geared up to follow him with a rousing call to arms.

He said nothing about it until right at the end. Everyone waited for the big moment. At last Callaghan beamed mischievously round the hall, mentioned the speculation, and said it reminded him of an

old music hall song, which he proceeded, to the fury of his hosts, to
sing:

'There was I
'Waiting at the church
'Waiting at the church
'Then I found he'd left me in the lurch ...'

And it ended:

'Can't get away to marry you today
'My wife won't let me.'

Union leaders knew, and Callaghan should have known, that the winter
was going to be a time of serious industrial strife. Union leaders had
tried hard to keep their side of the bargain they had made over pay
restraint, but could not hold back their increasingly radical members
any longer. Even the great Jack Jones, at his last Transport and General
Workers' Union (TGWU) conference, had not been able to hold the line,
and his successor Moss Evans said: 'If they did that to Jack Jones, just
imagine what they'd do to me.' It wasn't even worth trying. If Labour
was to have any chance at all, it needed to go to the country that
autumn. Callaghan delayed, and picked up all the unpopularity from
the so-called Winter of Discontent, paving the way for the Thatcher
victory of 1979.

But there was one more important political job for Gordon Brown to
do before that happened. The Scottish Labour executive chose him to
chair the committee running the campaign for a 'yes' vote in the devolution referendum which was to be held in 1979. It was an extraordinary
accolade for a young man of 28.

It was also, as he must have realised, a poison chalice. His party was
not united on the issue – Scottish Labour MPs, including Tam Dalyell,

were touring the country calling for a 'no' vote. Anti-devolutionists had managed to get into the Bill a stipulation that, for it to take effect, 40 per cent of the Scots electorate – not of those voting, but of the whole electorate – had to vote in favour. There was no way of stopping people using the referendum campaign to punish an unpopular and faltering government.

There were few resources for a campaign, and even fewer people willing to work on it. In the last seven days of the campaign Brown addressed 30 meetings. But by then he knew the mountain was too high. 32.8 per cent of those voting said yes, and 30.8 per cent said no. They had nowhere near 40 per cent of the entire electorate.

The Scottish National Party put down a motion of censure against the government, the Conservatives announced that they would support it, and after a night of frantic arm-twisting by his top lieutenants, the motion was carried by one vote and Callaghan's government fell. The failure of Brown's first big campaign brought about the end of the Labour government and the rise of Margaret Thatcher.

It had been valuable experience. He had seen the Labour Party divided, which was an unspeakably unpleasant sight and a very steep learning curve. Brown learned fast. He was in pole position to be elected scapegoat, yet managed not to be. During the campaign he met and got to know two of Labour's top power brokers in Scotland, John Smith and Donald Dewar, both of whom liked him, and he liked them.

Edinburgh South, which had returned a Tory even in October 1974, was not going to vote for Gordon Brown in 1979, but that did not stop the young candidate from putting his heart and soul into the battle. He defended the trade unions, opposing the tough new laws to govern their activity which the Conservatives wanted to introduce. He opposed his Tory opponent Michael Ancram's proposal for harsh new criminal laws: 'There is no evidence that stiffer penalties cut crime. I do not believe in being soft, but the idea that you can solve the problem by beating, flogging and hanging is complete nonsense.'

Nationally, the Conservatives won hands-down, with 339 seats and an overall majority of 44. In Scotland Labour did much better, winning 44 of the 71 seats, helped by the collapse of the SNP, and Brown reduced the Tory majority by 1,000 to only 2,460. To Brown, sitting in his Edinburgh flat, huge heaps of statistics and newspaper cuttings everywhere, contemplating at least four more years before he could enter Parliament, a job he was increasingly bored with, and a sense of emptiness where Margarita had once been, things seemed pretty bleak. But they were about to get better.

.

4

Between the Devil and the STV

As he became more high-profile in Scotland, Brown made valuable media contacts. Once the election was over, and it was clear he was going to be available for a while, Scottish Television offered him a job. There he quickly met a young woman who, for a time, was to take Margarita's place in his life, a journalist and Edinburgh University graduate called Sheena McDonald. She was forceful, able and ambitious, and unlike Margarita, seems not, at that stage anyway, to have contemplated spending her life with Brown. But they had a lot in common, both professionally and personally. Like him she was a child of the Manse – her father was a former moderator of the General Assembly of the Church of Scotland. The relationship ran its course, and she was succeeded in Brown's affections by the Glasgow-born lawyer Marion Caldwell, and later the public relations consultant Carol Craig.

Marion Caldwell was the longer-lasting affair: they maintained an on/off relationship for a decade or so. Tom Bower, Brown's most hostile biographer, says she was 'strung along' for all that time and she 'pandered to his demand for immediate attention whenever requested', but Brown's friends say the relationship was nothing like as unequal as Bower suggests, and Caldwell does not sound at all like the sort of woman who would have tolerated it. She was a successful lawyer, and is now an important figure in the Scottish legal establishment.

Television was a good training-ground for a politician with a tendency to have too many facts and figures at his fingertips, and to want to use all of them on every platform. As Brown himself told Paul

Routledge, 'TV is a very tough medium. You have to say what you want in a very short space of time. You have to say things succinctly to get your message across.' Tony Blair credits Gordon Brown with teaching him how to write press releases when they both entered Parliament in 1983, and STV is where Brown learned the skill himself.

Many politicians mishandle television. Some – Neil Kinnock and Menzies Campbell are two examples – do well in it at first, and are then unravelled by it. Brown's four years at STV taught him lessons many other politicians never fully understand.

He started as a producer on a political programme called *Ways and Means*, but moved quite quickly – perhaps because it is awkward to have an active politician working on a political programme – to be editor of a consumer programme, *What's Your Problem?*, which took up viewers' complaints. He added a sharp political edge to it by giving advice on how to claim benefits. A few well-regarded investigative programmes followed, including one called *Rags to Riches*, which showed that most of the North Sea oil companies had not paid Petroleum Revenue Tax.

He interviewed the former Prime Minister Edward Heath, with whom he got on well; and also met Labour's young rising star, Neil Kinnock, to whom he was introduced by the left-wing Labour MP Norman Buchan. Kinnock was in Edinburgh for an international rugby match, and came early to do a couple of meetings on the Thursday before the rest of the Welsh arrived.

Alongside all this there was another imperative in his life. If he wanted the right to call himself Dr Brown, he was running out of time to submit his thesis. He had been busy. He had held down a full time job, and spent evenings and weekends on his political work. His relationship with Margarita was one casualty of this lifestyle; he seems to have been determined that his PhD should not be another.

It's hard, at first, to see why this mattered to him. A PhD might have been useful if he wanted to return to academia, but he did not. A television journalist does not need a PhD, and neither does a politician. In fact, Labour politicians seem sometimes almost embarrassed by them. Dr John Reid refers scathingly to journalists with PhDs, as though it is some sort of disease, and resents anyone drawing attention to his. Brown himself does not use the title. So low-key is he about it that he is often referred to, incorrectly, as Mr Brown. But the thesis that earned him the right to call himself Dr Brown is a huge piece of detailed research, and represents years of work.

Perhaps it seemed a shame to waste the work done so far, but I do not think that was the real reason. The thesis itself, and even more his later biography of the old Scottish socialist hero Jimmy Maxton, read like a labour of love. He was deeply interested in Scottish labour history. I think Brown also believes that a person who aspires to help govern the country – and his ambition was already enormous – should have a strong feel for the past; and if he wants to rise through the Labour Party, he should know his labour history.

The thesis had to be in before ten years had elapsed from when he started it, and he made it, just: he delivered it in October 1981, with five minutes to spare. It's called *The Labour Party and Political Change in Scotland*, 1918–29. Like most PhD theses, it is long and rather dry, with pages and pages of references, and would mean little to someone who knew nothing of the period. But it is a serious, substantial and controversial contribution to labour history, comprehensively refuting Scottish labour's image of itself as the aristocracy of the movement. It repays study because the later Brown's prescriptions for his party are based to some extent on the expert and detailed understanding he had of its history.

'Labour never achieved its aim of becoming a mass membership party in Scotland,' he writes. 'At its peak the ILP [Independent Labour Party] which provided most of the Labour Party's individual members, had only 9,000 Scottish members. In 1929 this had dwindled to less than 5,000.' The ILP had been the organisation to which pre-First World War Labour MPs like Keir Hardie belonged, but after 1918 it became one element of the Labour Party, and as the Twenties and Thirties progressed, increasingly an element out on a left-wing limb. In Scotland in the 1920s, the ILP and the unions were the heart of Labour. The Labour Party itself hardly existed. Brown says that it was strongest in big industrial centres, where it drew strength from the unions, and it 'prospered or fell largely according to the strength of trade union activity'.

That was not a trap Brown intended the Labour Party to fall into in his generation. Labour must thrive even when the unions did not do so. The alternative was a recipe for non-achievement, for despite all the effort that went into labour organisation in the 1920s, 'most Scottish people were by 1929 little better housed, fed or economically secure than a decade before'. Scots suffered in the 1920s, with mass unemployment – worse than they had known before the First World War – and poverty. Yet Labour could not change this.

The lesson Brown learned is summed up in this inelegant but revealing sentence: 'Political life often exercises an independence that forbids an automatic equation between the existence of class divisions and either class consciousness, class conflict or a socialist consciousness.' In other words: poverty is often not radicalising, and politics does not always reflect people's real problems and concerns.

Neither was Scotland in those years in the vanguard of the labour movement, with a radical left-wing tradition. The image persists because the parliamentary left at the time was led by the Clydesiders, a group of committed left-wing MPs led by John Wheatley and James Maxton. But Brown shows that Scottish ILP members were moving towards Ramsay MacDonald and the centre ground, and away from Maxton and Wheatley, in the 1920s. By 1929, 'Maxton may have controlled the ILP in Britain: his base was being eroded in Scotland.' The ILP was 'the fulcrum of Labour Party activity in Scotland ... Almost all Labour Party candidates in 1929 were members of the ILP.' So the ILP's failings became the failings of Labour in Scotland. It was divided, its MPs were too far to the left of its members, and it exhausted itself in support of the miners during the 1926 General Strike.

Along the way, rather revealingly, Brown quotes with approval a passage from an academic essay by J Winter from the *Scottish Labour Historical Society Journal* of 1978. Winter is arguing that the nature of the Labour Party's socialism in the period was determined by the First World War, and he wrote: 'Clause 4 is incomprehensible outside the context.' Clause 4, of course, is the clause which Brown and Blair removed from Labour's constitution in 1994 and which Hugh Gaitskell had failed to remove 30 years earlier: the clause which committed Labour to 'public ownership of the means of production, exchange and control', which no Labour government or Labour leader had ever taken literally.

A much easier read is the spin-off from Brown's thesis, the biography of James Maxton, which he sat down and wrote as soon as the thesis had been delivered, and which was published by Mainstream in 1986. He had already spent many days in the home of Maxton's family. All Maxton's papers were stuffed in a trunk, unsorted. Brown would arrive, they would give him a cup of tea, and he would dive into them. They have now, partly on Brown's recommendation, gone to the Mitchell Library in Glasgow.

There must have been some political calculation in choosing Maxton as his subject. Maxton is almost a saint in Labour circles in Scotland. But though he does not say so in the book, Brown's father was connected with the Maxton circle, and had known James Barr, a fellow Presbyterian minister who became MP for Motherwell 1924–31, then for Coatbridge and Airdrie from 1935 until 1945. It's clear Brown was fascinated by Maxton, admired him, and he felt they had something in common.

On the face of it, that is odd. The Gordon Brown we know today is cautious to a fault. It's no accident that as soon as he used the word 'prudence' it stuck to him like a limpet. He is interested in power, not ideology, and he has taken almost endless trouble to dispense with ideological baggage, sometimes – as we shall see – to the point where the most dangerous charge against him is that he has acquired the ideological baggage of his political opponents.

Jimmy Maxton (1885–1945) was an idealist. What brought him into politics, the goad that drove him, was the poverty he saw on the Clyde. Socialism to him was the means by which the working class would break free from the shackles in which it had been bound by a brutal and unfair capitalist system.

However, the similarities are also startling, which is why, as Brown writes in his introduction, 'The story of Jimmy Maxton and of the Clydeside MPs who descended on Westminster in 1922 has fascinated me since I was a teenager.' He is too busy to look at the book much these days, but when he does he turns straight to the declaration they made about their intentions, as the huge press of Glaswegians came to St Enoch Station to cheer the Clydesiders on their way to London. He read it out to me: their promise to 'abjure vanity and self-aggrandisement, recognising that they are the honoured servants of the people and that their only righteous purpose is to promote the welfare of their fellow citizens and the well being of mankind'; to 'bear in their hearts the sorrows of the aged, the widowed mother and the poor that their lives shall not be without comfort'; to 'eradicate the corrupting effect of monopoly and avarice'. He sees a direct line of descent from the Presbyterians and Covenanters to the Clydesiders, and hearing him read the declaration, I imagine he is also hearing his father preaching.

Maxton's father, like Brown's, rose to the ranks of the professionals, in his case to become a headmaster – he was, as Brown wrote, 'a typical Scottish "lad o'pairts"', like Brown and Brown's father, and a devout Christian. Maxton's romantic appearance, like Brown's, was enhanced by long, flowing, jet-black hair. He grew up in at atmosphere of religion and social responsibility, and took a degree at Glasgow University, where he too edited the student magazine.

What attracted Brown to Maxton was the ILP leader's passion and idealism. But as Brown had pointed out in his earlier PhD thesis, by

1929 nothing had been done for the poor for whom all Maxton's energies and ability had been expended. After the fall of the Labour government in 1931, Maxton led his ILP out of the Labour Party and, as it turned out, into the wilderness. He was a great propagandist, he was loved in Scotland and in the House of Commons, but he was not what Robin Cook used to call 'a practical politician'. He had virtually no ambition for himself. He changed men's hearts, he gave them hope, but he did not change the world.

And what does our Chancellor and future Prime Minister think of that? He thinks it is admirable, but not enough. Here he is on Maxton in the 1930s: 'Now powerless in the country, Maxton was patronised in the House of Commons'. "The ruling class in this country have various ways of dealing with revolutionaries," wrote Kingsley Martin in 1933. "Where it cannot buy them off its usual method is flattery. But Maxton has refused the aristocratic embrace – he makes a rule of never dining with rich men – so they have found another way. They have made a House of Commons character of him ... They treat him as an institution and entertainment. It is a point of honour among them to appreciate Maxton's burning sincerity."'

Brown – though this is hardly mentioned in the book – does not think Maxton intended to become what he did become in the 1930s. He had hoped for real power, and was disappointed that Ramsay MacDonald did not include him in the 1924 government. Like Keir Hardie, Maxton sought to combine the Scottish radical and Christian traditions. 'He could not be bought. He never accepted hospitality he could not return and was unimpressed by all social distinctions. Although he owned up to his Glasgow MA he turned down an offer in 1930 of an honorary degree from Edinburgh University. He had little interest in material possessions.'

By the time the book was published in 1986, its author was a rising Labour MP. It is a good biography, by far the best thing available on this important and interesting political figure. But we are in the odd position where the biographer is already a far more significant political figure than his subject ever was, and modern readers can be forgiven for reading it more for what it tells us about its author than what it tells us about its subject.

Gordon Brown's sense of Labour history has Maxton as the right man for one stage – the stage of education and agitation. Brown now sees the Thirties, after Maxton's glory days, as the time when Maynard Keynes, Lloyd George, and even Oswald Mosley, were searching for a new way forward – and he sometimes quotes Nye Bevan asking Jennie Lee whether she wants to be pure and impotent, or to change the world. I think he sees Attlee as the man for another stage, and himself as the man for this stage.

As he wrote the book, Brown was watching the Labour Party, 50 years on, tearing itself to pieces. He must have been struck by the parallels with Maxton's time. The Bennites were not, of course, Maxton's ILP, Tony Benn was never revered the way Jimmy Maxton was, and Brown never had anything like the respect for Benn that he had for Maxton, but some of his criticisms of the two would be the same: that their ideological purity prevented them from changing anything in the real world. There was a sense in which the Labour Party battle had always been the same one, whether the left was led by Maxton in the 1920s and early 1930s, Stafford Cripps in the late 1930s, Nye Bevan in the 1940s and 1950s, or Tony Benn in the 1980s.

The 1979–83 split was worse than earlier battles. The younger Bennites – Benn's acolytes more than Benn himself – had a kind of grinding self-righteousness, and were quite happy to spend their lives in the arid bureaucratic work of manipulating Labour's constitution, in a way that Maxton's and Bevan's supporters would have scorned. In their own terms, they succeeded. In 1980 Labour's conference took the choice of leader out of the hands of MPs, and decided there was to be an electoral college consisting of three elements: MPs, trade unions, and ordinary members. But it did not decide on the exact proportions that would go to each of these three elements. That decision was postponed to a special conference in the new year.

It was a disaster for Labour. First, the delay meant that the bitter internal quarrel about the proportions absorbed the party's energies, and baffled and alienated the voters, for months. Second, both the unions and the Labour Party could only be damaged by the unions' role as political power-brokers being made both stronger and more high-profile – they have suffered grievously for this bout of egoistical self-indulgence ever since.

Brown, like the young Neil Kinnock, saw the gaping abyss. Kinnock begged fellow left wingers to worry more about getting rid of Margaret Thatcher than getting rid of right wingers in the Labour Party. Callaghan, Kinnock insisted, was guilty of 'timidity, not treachery', and 'fifty years of Callaghan is better than one year of Thatcher.'[1]

Worse was to come. When the special conference met, at Wembley in January 1981, a classic trade-union fix went wrong and handed outright victory to the Bennites, who wanted, and got, 40 per cent of the votes for the unions, with 30 per cent for MPs and 30 per cent for ordinary Labour Party members. It was the worst possible result, casting the trade unions in the role of arrogant power-brokers and lending credibility to the Tory charge that union leaders ran the country under Labour.

By then, Callaghan had resigned. The left were furious, believing he had gone early in order to ensure that his successor was elected by the old system – that is, by Labour MPs alone. He probably did, but it did not have the desired effect. Michael Foot was elected Labour leader at the age of 67, beating the front-runner and Callaghan's preferred successor Denis Healey by 139 votes to 129.

To many Labour people Foot's election seemed like a dream come true. They indulged in a brief daydream of a new sort of Prime Minister; a human being, who did not have the politician's polish, who could wear a less-than-perfect overcoat at the Cenotaph (and did, to a loud chorus of media condemnation), who was passionate about ideas and determined to turn them into policy, who was also a writer of distinction, not just about politics but also about such people as Byron and H G Wells.

It was a false dawn. Our politicians over the next quarter-century were to look more and more like grey-suited purpose-built machines. The bibliophile leader seems increasingly an anachronism. Brown in 2007 will be the first Prime Minister of literary distinction since Harold Macmillan, and it is no coincidence that today he is the 94-year-old Michael Foot's closest friend in the government. Nor is it coincidence that Sue Nye, who started out as Foot's assistant in 1980, is today Gordon Brown's chief adviser and gatekeeper.

In 1980 Brown, along with Neil Kinnock, briefly shared that daydream. But Foot the veteran Bevanite spent two unrewarding years fighting the sharp-toothed Bennites, who seemed determined to destroy any lingering chance of the daydream coming true. Their hunger for constitutional tinkering within the Labour Party bears an uncanny similarity to the hunger of the Blairites after Blair was elected leader in 1994, and it is surprising how many of the Bennites in 1980 were Blairites by 1994.

They had convinced Labour's conference of the need for all Labour MPs to be re-selected after each election, so that they could if necessary be de-selected, and were encouraging constituency left-wingers to dump right-wing Labour MPs.

Foot's position was immeasurably weakened in January 1981 when four prominent right-wingers – Roy Jenkins, David Owen, Shirley Williams and Bill Rodgers – left the Labour Party and founded the Social Democratic Party. Two months later Benn announced that he would challenge the incumbent, Denis Healey, for the more or less meaningless post of deputy leader of the Labour Party. The Bennites said the new election machinery needed to be 'tested', to which Neil Kinnock responded that this was 'a bit like Christmas morning when a kid's given a watch and starts taking it apart to see how it works'. But arguing against an election was not easy, for the younger Bennites took to saying, rather nastily: 'So you're against democracy, are you?' Arthur Scargill, the rising Bennite in the National Union of Mineworkers, ratcheted up the stakes by saying that those who did not support Benn were wreckers of everything Labour stood for.

Since Benn was determined to stand, John Silkin from the 'soft' left also agreed to stand, in effect to wreck Benn's campaign. He knew there were MPs who did not want to vote for Benn, but would face deselection if they voted for Healey, and he offered them a way out – an anti-Benn left-winger.

This set the scene for Labour's dreadful summer in 1981. All three candidates did the rounds of union conferences, and the publicity they attracted ensured that trade unions came to be seen as far more powerful and authoritarian than they really were, with disastrous long term consequences for them. By the end of the summer, when Healey narrowly squeaked home, the next election was already probably lost, and the Labour Party was in a state of civil war.

Foot was the wrong man to battle the Bennites because he shared their distrust of strong leadership. His biographer Kenneth Morgan places him as 'the natural heir of [Keir] Hardie and [George] Lansbury, if not quite of the firebrand Jimmy Maxton' – who was opposed to leadership. 'Much of Foot's career had been a battle with the whips and successive leaders against the constraints of party discipline.'[2] He knew it had to be done, if a generation of Thatcherism was to be averted, but it was not what he was good at. And a generation of Thatcherism was not averted.

That was not for want of effort by Foot's strongest supporter on Labour's Scottish executive, Gordon Brown, who was 29 when Foot became leader. Life in the Scottish Labour Party turned into a grinding series of constitutional confrontations, and on the Scottish executive, Gordon Brown led one army, and George Galloway, later MP for Glasgow Hillhead and now Respect MP for Bethnal Green, led the other. It was

Brown's introduction to machine politics. Before then, he voted on the executive on the merits of the issue. Now he voted with a bloc. He had learned the harsh lesson that that is how to get things done in politics.

The embattled Michael Foot was present for one of these confrontations on 14 November 1981. Galloway launched into a furious attack on him for denying Benn his support for the shadow cabinet, and on Denis Healey for his views on nuclear disarmament (unlike Foot, Healey was not in favour of unilateral nuclear disarmament). Brown weighed in in Foot's defence, pointing out the obvious fact that in order to achieve anything at all, Labour had to win the support of the voters. 'Anything which prevents this and which puts the relationship between the party and the trade unions in jeopardy is not only needless but harmful.' The meeting ended acrimoniously. The Scottish Labour Party, like its counterpart south of the border, had divided into two armed camps, and they loathed each other.

There was still just the faintest chance that Labour might win the next general election, because unemployment was rising under the Thatcher government, which was increasingly unpopular. That faint chance was snuffed out when Argentina under General Galtieri invaded the Falkland Islands, and was driven out by British forces. Margaret Thatcher the war leader could not be beaten, certainly not by a divided and faction-ridden Labour Party.

What worried Gordon Brown about the next general election, even more than whether Labour could win, was whether it would see him into Parliament for a safe seat which would be the bedrock of a political career. Television was all very well, and he enjoyed it, but it was not what he wanted to do with his life. He wanted real power, not the appearance of power which journalists enjoy. He did not want to fight the near-hopeless Edinburgh South again.

He was doing all the right things. He was well respected on the Scottish executive, and well in with the Transport and General Workers

Union (TGWU) which could deliver the nomination in several Scottish Labour constituencies. He had impressed all the key power-brokers in the Scottish Labour Party. And when, early in 1983, Dunfermline East came up, he was well placed to go for the nomination.

There was a strong Communist tradition in this coalmining constituency close to Edinburgh. Its borders were very close to those of the constituency which had been represented by Communist MP Willie Gallacher from 1935 to 1950, and there was still a Communist on the local council. Brown needed – and secured – the support of the key TGWU man in Scotland, the Communist Hugh Wyper. By the time of the selection meeting, a combination of TGWU influence and lobbying by Brown's supporters, including a clever Scottish Labour lawyer called Charles Falconer, had pretty well ensured Brown's victory on the first ballot.

Brown's standing was further enhanced during the 1983 general election. In his constituency, where there was high unemployment, he campaigned on jobs, telling the voters that Labour's principal aim was to cut unemployment to a million within five years. As a national figure in Scotland – 1983 was his year as chairman of the Scottish Labour Party executive – he grabbed headlines for his accusation that Thatcher had ordered the shredding of documents to hide her real agenda. This, he said, included 'abolishing mortgage tax relief, abandoning the wages councils [which ensured a minimum wage in low-paid industries], ending the present system of child benefit, and forcing everyone to take up private medical insurance – with charges for visits to the doctor under consideration.' They also planned to decimate the coal industry, he said, shedding 10,000 jobs in Scotland.

Brown's substantial victory – he was elected with 18,515 votes, a majority of 11,301 over his nearest rival – did not make him at all cheerful. On the night of polling day, 9 June 1983, he was utterly depressed by the huge scale of Labour's defeat. The new House of Commons would contain 396 Conservative MPs, 209 Labour ones and 26 from the alliance of the Liberal Party and the new Social Democratic Party. And the voting figures showed that things were even worse. The Conservatives polled 43.5 per cent of the votes, with 28.3 for Labour and 26 per cent for the Alliance. Labour had almost been pushed into third place – and if it had been, that was a position from which the party could hardly have recovered.

5

An Instant Parliamentary Star

'The trouble with Gordon,' the former Labour MP Oona King once said, 'is that he's all substance and no style.' It's a common perception, and it isn't true. As so often happens with politicians, he has been overtaken by his image, which is that of a dour and ferociously clever Scotsman, lacking in media skills and unable to connect with people, contrasting with the smiling Tony Blair, who understands the media, is good on television, and has plenty of style but is short of substance.

But when the two first met, after they were both elected to Parliament for the first time at the June 1983 general election and shared a small, windowless office in the bowels of the Palace of Westminster, it was the other way round. It was Brown the former television producer who knew his way around the media, who knew how to write press releases and what a sound bite was, and what to wear and what not to wear for television. It was Brown the seasoned politician who knew how to relate to his parliamentary colleagues, and who could explain what was needed to Blair the awkward ingénue. It was Brown who knew how to defuse situations with a well-timed witticism. It was Brown who had the instinctive charm that won friends. Blair hungrily learned from his older and more experienced mentor. 'My press releases were like essays before Gordon showed me how to write them,' he said later. The two young MPs liked each other at once, and it was Brown again who led the way on the first big decision they had to make: to support Neil Kinnock's bid to succeed Michael Foot as Labour's leader.

For Brown it was natural. He and Kinnock were fellow rugby and soccer fanatics who had enjoyed watching internationals together ever since they first met in Scotland towards the end of the 1970s – Kinnock describes Brown today as 'an encyclopaedic sports fan, just as he's encyclopaedic about everything that interests him – he knows about people's backgrounds, who played, what the score was, why the score was that.' And Brown had spent some years positioning himself on what was known then as the 'soft left', led in Parliament by Kinnock and his campaign manager Robin Cook. The soft left considered itself to the left of the old Wilson/Callaghan regime, represented in this leadership election by Kinnock's main opponent Roy Hattersley, but it did not share the rigid doctrinal certainties of the Bennites.

For Blair, Kinnock was a less obvious choice. Blair did not have anything like Brown's experience of Labour politics, but such as it was, he would have seemed more a natural Hattersley man. Two things probably changed his mind. One was the advocacy of Gordon Brown and Blair's old Islington friend Charles Clarke. The other was the fact that Kinnock was clearly going to win, and in politics it is always good to be on the winning side.

Kinnock was going to win because the big unions supported him. The 1983 leadership election was the first in which the unions played a direct role. As soon as the general election was done with, white collar union leader Clive Jenkins casually announced that Michael Foot was resigning and his union's support was going to Neil Kinnock to be Foot's successor. 'I'm not standing for leader,' said Denis Healey on television. 'Can you blame me, when it's all apparently been carved up in advance by a few trade union leaders?'

Jenkins was one half of a powerful trade union duo of Welsh trade union leaders known as 'the Taffia' – the other was the TGWU's Moss Evans. A flamboyant man who never saw any reason to be coy about being seen to exercise power, he managed, three days after the general election, simultaneously to fire the starting gun in the race for the next leader, and announce the winner. It made the unions look as though their first concern was politics, which lost them members; and it made the Labour Party look like a stooge for union leaders, which cost it votes. Brown and Kinnock went along with this – there was not much else to be done – but they could see, as Clive Jenkins could not, the long term damage the unions were doing, as they had in the deputy leadership election, by flexing their political muscles. They were focusing unwanted attention on the block vote.

Brown owed his selection to the trade unions. It was not quite as crude an operation as Tony Blair's in Sedgefield, but it was an old-fashioned trade union fix nonetheless. But in 1983 he already knew that something had to be done. Some of the more astute union leaders, like John Edmonds of the GMB, saw that they were turning the Labour Party and the unions into millstones round each others' necks, and Edmonds and Kinnock began urgent discussions about a new sort of relationship.

As leader, Kinnock put Brown on the committee debating the government's Trade Union Bill, working under Brown's old Edinburgh friend and mentor John Smith, now the shadow Employment Minister. Brown held – and still holds – the now-unfashionable view that trade unions are an indispensable part of work in a civilised society, and that without strong unions, his constituents are powerless in the face of the greediest employer. He knew the unions, and he liked them. He was on the committee in order to fight, line by line, the government's intention to take away the unions' power to protect working people – for that is how Brown and most Labour people saw the Bill. He called it 'a disguised attempt to cut wages'. It also sought to force them to hold ballots before giving money to the Labour Party, which, said Brown, might have been fair enough if it had also demanded a ballot of shareholders before companies gave money to the Conservative Party. Privately, he knew that the Bill would go through despite his efforts, and Labour had better become less dependent on trade union money. It should start to get its hands on some of the company money which could be handed over rather more easily. Gordon Brown was always a prudent Scot, especially where money was concerned.

But there was a tightrope to walk: for at the same time, he wanted to reduce the unions' power in Labour Party politics, and he could see ahead of him the rumbling of the great industrial disputes of the early eighties which were to bring the era of seventies trade union power and influence to a very sudden and bruising end. Brown saw the unions – as, at their best, they saw themselves – as a bulwark against poverty and exploitation. Poverty, as he had seen it in Kirkcaldy as a child and in his constituency as an MP, was his biggest political concern, and his first parliamentary speech was about social security, a big issue in Dunfermline East, with its high levels of unemployment. The speech was a *tour de force*: detailed, passionate, carefully prepared, the speech of a new member who is determined to make his mark.

There were 8,000 people claiming supplementary benefit in his constituency, he said, which meant that 15,000 men, women and children were dependent on means-tested benefits. In Scotland as a whole, more than a million people – one in five of the population – lived at or below the government's poverty line. 'This is all because the government's philosophy is that the rich must get rich by way of tax cuts and that the poor must become poorer to ensure true prosperity.' Yet benefit levels were dwindling to something like those of the hungry 1930s.

All this work was to mean nothing. Everything Neil Kinnock and his friends fought for in 1983 was smashed to pieces by the 1984–5 miners strike. The government wanted a massive programme of pit closures, and the leader of the National Union of Mineworkers, Arthur Scargill, believed he could halt the programme and bring down the government by calling a nationwide strike on 1 March 1984, at the start of the summer when coal stocks were high, without balloting his members. It was the miners' misfortune that, just as the greatest crisis of their union's proud history arose, they elected the worst leader in their history. Exactly a year later, his once united union terminally split, his once wealthy and strong organisation ruined and powerless, Scargill led the tattered remnants of his troops back to work, defeated, demoralised, and desperately poor.

There was nothing Brown could do. Scargill's behaviour undercut everything he tried to do to mitigate the effect of the anti-trade union laws. He knew Scargill should have held a ballot, but could not say so because it would seem like he was attacking the miners. The publicity destroyed his and Kinnock's efforts to make the Labour Party sound sensible and reasonable. He could not even do much for the mining families in his own constituency, though his surgery was full of striking miners and their wives in dreadful hardship. The government had taken away their social security payments, and was deducting £15 a week from benefits payable to their wives and children to make up for strike pay from the union, even though it knew the union could not pay it. He did his best for them – he made speeches, he appealed to the social security minister, he begged and pleaded, then stormed, and achieved nothing. The government was going to win – and win so soundly that no other union was going to place its members in harm's way. He earned the respect of his own mining communities for his work to try to help them, the speeches he made, the lobbying he did. He took some satisfaction in the small things he could do for them as a constituency MP.

Brown liked running his surgery. Many MPs see this as a chore, but to Brown it had similarities with what his father did as a minister. Constituency work done well is about helping people who are downtrodden and defeated by the system. To this day Brown will boast of a woman who came to him because her wages were not enough to live on; he found she was not being paid properly, took her case to the relevant wages council, and got her pay increased to the proper level. But he knew – everyone in the Labour Party knew – that the unions and the Labour Party had to change, far more radically than most people yet understood.

The work of attacking Thatcherism still had to be done, and Brown did it with more talent and grace than most. The skills learned in television were deployed day after day, both in finding and dramatically revealing confidential information, and in showing himself to be the master of the telling phrase. With wages the lowest in Europe, and low wages and high unemployment an instrument of policy, he wanted to know: 'How much poorer have people to become to secure true prosperity for all?'

It was only a matter of time before this obviously rising star became one of the first of the 1983 intake to be offered a front bench job. Amazingly, in November 1984 he turned down the first offer that came his way, to be a member of the Scottish Office team, fearing being corralled forever in Scottish politics. Twenty minutes after Brown left his puzzled leader's office, Kinnock saw Tony Blair and offered him a place in Labour's treasury team under Roy Hattersley. Rather more conventionally, Blair jumped at the chance.

That decision tells us a lot about Gordon Brown. He always carefully examines the teeth of any gift horse that comes his way, and he did not turn a hair as he threw away a chance that most politicians of 33, with less than two years in the House of Commons, would have given anything for. He knew who he was and where he wanted to go, which was to the top in national politics. He had a certainty and self-confidence at 33 that most people do not acquire until much later in life, if at all. It never seems to have occurred to Brown that the chance might not come again.

And of course it did come, a year later when Kinnock made him a front bench spokesman in the trade and industry team, with special responsibility for regional policy under his old friend John Smith. It was exactly the niche he wanted, allowing him to speak on the things he knew and cared most about.

So for the rest of that Parliament he took the jobs campaign to the country, while Kinnock fought to reposition Labour in the mainstream and weaken the grip of the Bennites and of Militant while giving Labour a more professional campaigning style. It was necessary, but not sufficient. On 11 June 1987, Margaret Thatcher swept back into Downing Street with an majority of 102.

new

new Labour
because **Britain**
deserves better

6

The Next Prime Minister?

I f anyone had doubted that Brown was one of the Parliamentary
Labour Party's brightest rising stars and probably a future leader,
such doubt was laid to rest soon after the 1987 general election. He
was elected to the Shadow Cabinet, its youngest member, a remarkable
accolade for so new an MP. There were 15 members to be elected, and
Brown came 11th. Tony Blair did pretty well too – he just missed election, coming 17th.

Of course it was partly machine politics. They were both on the
Tribune slate (the Tribune Group had been the left wing of the Parliamentary Labour Party, but by then it was increasingly attracting mainstream figures like Blair and Brown). And to get on that, they had to be
on a secret slate for the slate.. This was compiled before the Tribune
Group met by Nick Brown, a former trade union official and another
of the 1983 intake. Nonetheless, the result showed how far these two
clever young men had progressed in a short time.

Another sign of their status was Kinnock's decision to entrust them
with a delicate mission. Roy Hattersley wanted to give up being deputy
leader. He had never wanted the job, and only took it out of duty.
Kinnock asked Blair and Brown to persuade Hattersley that his duty
was not over. They told Hattersley they could promise the support of
the Tribune group of left wing MPs. Then Blair said something extraordinary: 'I mean real Tribunites, not people like Gordon and I, who felt
we had to join.' What Brown felt about this frank piece of cynicism is
not recorded.[1]

Hattersley asked to be moved from shadowing the exchequer to shadowing home affairs. He was replaced as Shadow Chancellor by John Smith, and Brown became Smith's deputy – Shadow Chief Secretary, with a seat in the Shadow Cabinet. He was well pleased with this, as well he might be. He probably never knew that he almost did far better. Neil Kinnock's papers reveal that, in the first draft of his Shadow Cabinet thinking, in which John Smith would have been Shadow Foreign Secretary, Gordon Brown was pencilled in at defence. In the second draft he would have got energy. Blair, though not in the Shadow Cabinet, was given responsibility for relations with the City of London.

Brown was also to play a key part in the policy rethink that Kinnock and his advisers believed was needed if Labour was ever to win again. The strategy was decided by Kinnock and Charles Clarke. They thought that neither their policy nor their communications had worked; but since the press seemed to think their communications had worked, they should go along with this myth. Therefore, they decided, they must change the policies but keep the spin doctors.

This had a long-term consequence the implications of which were not understood by any of the players at the time. It marks the real point at which the balance of power between Gordon Brown and Tony Blair started, very slowly, to change. Although neither Kinnock nor Clarke believed Labour's communications chief Peter Mandelson to be the miracle-worker which others thought him, the fact that others did think that meant that the Tories feared him, and this fear, they decided, must be encouraged. It followed that they had to build up Mandelson's power. It was this power, in the end, that was used to make Blair, and not Brown, party leader 11 years later.

For the moment, though, the man who felt the chill was the Shadow Trade and Industry Secretary, Bryan Gould. Just as he was about to send his report for the policy review to the printer, Blair and Brown walked unannounced into his office, accompanied by Kinnock's economic adviser John Eatwell. 'They felt,' Gould writes, 'that the policy should not go forward in its present form. They objected in particular to what remained of any commitment to return privatised industries to some form of public ownership, and the formula agreed for purchasing the 2 per cent shareholding in British Telecom which would give the Labour government a majority shareholding.'[2]

Gould was furious at being asked to change his report so late in the day, and refused, even though he had little doubt that it was Kinnock's voice he was hearing. It was effectively the end of what had, until then, looked like a glittering political career. Mandelson let it be known that Gould was on the down escalator, and Mandelson proved to be right, as he generally was about such matters.

Mandelson's friends and contemporaries Tony Blair and Gordon Brown were on the up escalator, and Mandelson made sure people knew that, too. Brown and Blair knew Mandelson's importance and influence, and watched the way he first promoted, then junked Bryan Gould. They knew Mandelson was an important friend and a dangerous enemy.

Mandelson admired both Blair and Brown enormously. Who would he choose, if he ever had to choose between them? It looks as though, quite early on, he found himself more at ease with the relaxed, boyish Blair than the intellectual workaholic Brown.

What the three had in common was a certainty that Labour would never again hold office unless it broke decisively with the Attlee settlement of Britain's affairs. They believed they must abandon the idea of the mixed economy, in which certain industries, especially natural monopolies like railways, water and electricity were in public hands; and that the welfare state would have to have a greater private sector input. The political centre of gravity had shifted, and unless Labour shifted with it, the Party was finished.

But their emotional reactions to this intellectual conclusion were radically different. Blair had no emotional connection to Labour's history, and cared little for trade unions. Mandelson had a complicated connection with his party's history: his grandfather Herbert Morrison was a key member of the Attlee cabinet between 1945 and 1951, and had always believed that he, and not Attlee, should have been Prime Minister. He was sure Attlee went too far down the road of socialist reform, and was the first person, in the 1950s just before Mandelson was born, to call for Labour to 'modernise' – the word which Mandelson and Blair have made famous for our generation. Morrison meant by it very much the same things as his grandson meant, nearly half a century later: trying, as Mandelson once put it in a private letter to Roy Hattelsey, not to sound too committed to the 'have-nots', for fear of alienating the 'haves'. Mandelson seemed almost to glory in the conclusion that most of Labour's past needed jettisoning.

By contrast, Brown's connection with Labour history was organic. An upbringing in the Manse, with its public service ideals, rubbing shoulders with real poverty; student politics in the radical Sixties; years in Scottish Labour politics; a PhD thesis on Scottish labour history; writing the biography of Jimmy Maxton; after all that, he was to advocate policies which would make Maxton turn in his grave.

But he thought the conclusions inescapable. He spent the summer of 1988 in the Harvard University library, looking at the reasons for the USA's economic success, and came back with the germ of an economic philosophy which he thought included the best of the left – a concern to help the underdog, and not to permit extreme poverty – with what he increasingly saw as the dynamism of American capitalism.

'I was trying,' he told Paul Routledge, 'to find a solution to the problem of poverty that was quite different to what we had done before, because I knew our tax and spend policies were not popular – and they were not tackling the problem of poverty. The difficulty was to find a new way forward. It was quite important to me in the years I was Shadow Chief Secretary to get Labour attuned to the global economy, but to make sure in the global economy we didn't create a nation of people who were marginalised and lost out.'

He was the thinker of the three, and – most people would have said – the future Prime Minister. Neil Kinnock says: 'Until the 1992 election my assumption had been that if we had formed the government in 1992 my successor would be Gordon, and if we lost the election then John Smith's successor would be Gordon. From 1988 to 1992, in terms of political prominence and huge capacity, Gordon was absolutely striking. In terms of exposure, performance in the House of Commons, recognition in the Party and the country, everyone knew Gordon was a very considerable figure.'

Margaret Thatcher's majority was still too large, and Labour's internal divisions too deep, for the 1987 parliament to be anything other than a constant, grinding battle for Labour's leaders. What Brown could do was watch and learn, and Brown was good at that. He watched Margaret Thatcher using her economic adviser Sir Alan Walters to undermine her Chancellor, Nigel Lawson, and he knew that if he were ever Chancellor – a post he might well hold one day – he would not let that happen to him. Tony Blair's economic adviser Derek Scott never had the chance to be an Alan Walters. He became frustrated at his lack of influence and eventually resigned and wrote a book attacking Brown.

In the autumn of 1988, John Smith suffered a serious heart attack, and Brown stood in for him while he was off work. His first big test was the reply to Nigel Lawson's autumn statement in November. It was a big chance for a young politician, and Brown rose to the occasion. The Chancellor's pledge to bring inflation down to zero was brought back to torment him, as was the worsening balance of payments. 'Is there anything more revealing of the government's priorities,' Brown asked, 'than the fact that when the Chancellor went to the Conservative Party conference to affirm a new round of top rate tax cuts for those who are already rich, he still refuses to find even the tiny amount that would save free eyesight tests and free dental checkups, even for pensioners?'

It was a fine performance, and Brown's reward came quickly in the

Shadow Cabinet elections. He topped the poll, with his mentor John Smith coming second – and he was still only 37. Blair was elected for the first time, in ninth place. Brown stayed in his Treasury job. Blair became Energy spokesman, with the task of opposing the government's plans for electricity privatisation.

Smith made the occasional telephone call from hospital to his friend, the deputy leader Roy Hattersley. Smith was torn between wanting to see his young protégé do well, and worrying ever so slightly that he might do so well that no one would be pleased to see Smith back. Hattersley says: 'I told him: Gordon is managing it with complete efficiency and complete loyalty.' As Smith started to recover, Brown made the occasional weekend trip to Scotland to help him climb the great hills known as The Munroes, a form of exercise designed to aid his boss's recovery.

When Smith came back, in January 1989, Hattersley took Brown to lunch and told him that his performance had earned him the right to consideration for pretty well any Shadow Cabinet post he liked. Brown replied that Smith would want him around at first to lighten the load, so he thought he should stay where he was. Hattersley was full of admiration for this sense of duty, and still is today.

Union leader John Edmonds, who saw a lot of the policy review meetings, says: 'Brown deferred constantly to Smith, who was in total command of economic policy. But Smith liked Brown very much, and told me so often. He treated him like a much loved family member. He laughed about him said he still acted like a student, comes to meetings with the contents of four filing cabinets and drops half of them before the meeting starts.' Brown in those days, says Edmonds, had a black pen with which he scrawled on everything, jabbing so hard that sometimes he thought the pen was going through the table.

The final policy review package, unveiled later that year, owed a lot to Brown's new thinking. It included higher rates of tax to be capped at 50 pence in the pound; better child benefit; a charter of employee rights; but no repeal of much of the Conservatives' anti-union legislation. Unilateral nuclear disarmament was decisively junked, and Europe embraced. Tony Benn called it 'by far the most right wing policy during my time in the Party'.

And with the review out, Labour's demons slain, the party ahead in the polls, and the government unpopular and in disarray, the future looked about as good as a rising young politician could hope for. Thatcher and Lawson obliged by falling out terminally over key aspects of economic policy and Lawson gave up the unequal struggle with Sir Alan Walters for the Prime Minister's ear, resigning and tormenting his tormentor. Brown tormented both of them, to great effect.

Meanwhile Brown and Smith were winning the battle to commit Labour to joining the Exchange Rate Mechanism against Bryan Gould, whose painful decline continued with Brown taking his job as shadow trade and industry spokesman. A Kinnock government, with Smith and Brown running the economy, looked a very likely prospect for 1992.

Unfortunately, the Tories thought so too, and took the only effective action they could have taken. They dumped Margaret Thatcher, elected the uncharismatic but likeable John Major to succeed her and scrapped the unpopular Community Charge, better known as the 'Poll Tax'. The idea that everyone should pay exactly the same for local services, whether they were multi-millionaires or on the breadline, was a Thatcherite step too far. There was, briefly, talk of a similar coup in the Labour Party to replace Kinnock, probably with Smith though, amazingly, Brown's name was also mentioned. It came to nothing, partly because Smith and Brown played it very straight, making it clear they were not interested.

At Labour's conference Brown's attack on the new Prime Minister was easily the most effective. Parts of it have a remarkably contemporary feel. 'In his first 100 days, President Bush told him what to do. In his second 100 days, President Bush told him what to do. In his third 100 days, the photographers told him what to do.' If you did not know which Prime Minister this was said of, I do not think your first guess would be John Major.

The delegates knew it would be the last conference before the election, and wanted to give the leadership the best start they could. Brown gave them the chance: effective tirades against the government, a few memorable jokes (the Tories, he said, now depended on dubious foreign donations, 'most shameful of all, on a Greek billionaire moving his money out of colonels and into majors'); and some policies which at least looked like things the Labour Party has traditionally applauded: a national investment bank, tougher controls on the city, plans for upgrading skills. Labour entered the election campaign marginally ahead in the polls, and then, somehow, lost. John Major returned to Downing Street with an overall majority of 21 seats.

And that defeat, even today, is the wound the Labour Party still touches, and finds that it still hurts. Even today, they will fall out about why it happened and whose fault it was. There are those who say it was all John Smith's fault for producing a shadow budget which could be unfairly characterised by the Conservatives as 'tax and spend'. Those who say this are generally Blairites, but Gordon Brown has some sympathy with it. Then there are those who say it was all the fault of the Sheffield Rally – a great, vulgar, triumphalist television spectacular a couple of days before the election, the brainchild of Peter Mandelson, which spectacularly misfired and made Labour sound triumphalist and Kinnock sound threatening.

Others – Roy Hattersley is one of these – place much of the blame on the decision to discuss proportional representation a week before polling day, and therefore appear to be offering a bribe to the Liberal Democrats. And there are those who blame Labour's spin machine. Mandelson had left his job as head of communications to be Labour candidate for Hartlepool, but meddled fatally with his old staff. For two years Labour's communications were destroyed by personal and political infighting. When it came to the election, Labour had the worst of both worlds: a reputation as an invincible spin machine, and the reality of a completely ineffective one.

The bitter, protracted recriminations started soon after 11 p.m. that night, when the result came through from Basildon in Essex. Basildon was exactly the sort of seat Labour needed to win. Gordon Brown, for one, knew the worst as soon as he heard the Basildon result, and he was utterly depressed.

There never was much doubt that Kinnock would go quickly, and John Smith would succeed him. Smith, according to Roy Hattersley, thought Kinnock might try to engineer the succession for Bryan Gould, to whom Kinnock was personally much closer than he was to Smith. He was mistaken. Kinnock had no such intention. And there were, once again, those who thought that the leadership should go to the rising star of the new generation – Gordon Brown. Blair wanted Brown to run. 'Blair felt that the swift election of Smith would be the end of the modernising project' says John Carr, a close Blair associate at the time. Blair tried hard to persuade Brown to stand against Smith.[3]

But Brown never considered standing. At all the critical moments of his career, you always see this: if it is not quite the right time, it is not quite right, and that is all there is to it. He would not fight for the parliamentary nomination in Hamilton in his mid-twenties even though fighting hard might just secure it, and enable him to leapfrog contemporaries, for it was not the right time or place. He would not take Kinnock's offer of a front-bench job when new to parliament, for it was not the right job. And he would not give a moment's consideration to running against John Smith for the leadership. It was time for loyalty to his old boss, to whom he owed a lot. He could only do harm by standing.

It was an instinct which Tony Blair, who was still, at that time, probably Brown's closest political friend, did not share or understand. Two years later, in 1994, when Brown stood down in Blair's favour, Blair thought that Brown had no real grounds for complaint – for his moment had come in 1992, and he had inexplicably chosen to pass it up. Had it been Blair, and not Brown, who stood just a chance of defeating Smith in 1992, he would have had a go. But Blair was not credible in 1992. Brown was, just. Blair never understood why Brown did not throw his hat into the ring. 'He chickened out', was Blair's contemptuous verdict.[4]

Smith was elected leader, and he and Neil Kinnock were sure that he would be Prime Minister after the next general election – though Brown was less sure, and Blair very doubtful. Brown became Shadow Chancellor, and Blair Shadow Home Secretary. Smith offered Blair the foreign affairs portfolio, and Blair was attracted to the idea, but Brown gave him some sober career advice, that being Shadow Home Secretary would earn him more kudos.

On 16 September 1992, the Chancellor of the Exchequer Norman Lamont struggled to support the pound in an old-fashioned devaluation crisis, eventually announcing the suspension of Britain's membership of the European Exchange Rate Mechanism. By then almost £10 billion, 40 per cent of the national reserves, had been squandered in a vain attempt to buy sterling out of trouble. The Conservatives' reputation for good economic management was in tatters, and, as their split over Europe turned into an abyss, they never recovered in the opinion polls or looked like a party capable of winning the next general election.

Brown and Blair travelled to Washington in January 1993 for talks with President Clinton's staff – many of their meetings being arranged by a then unknown young *Financial Times* journalist called Ed Balls, now the Financial Secretary to the Treasury and tipped for big things under Prime Minister Brown. They discussed American economic management, and how Middle America had been won for the Democrats as they were sure Middle England had to be won for Labour.

At the October Labour Party conference that year, John Smith slayed the last of the Old Labour dragons he thought worth slaying, winning reforms that ensured the Labour leader, and Labour MPs, would be chosen by a system of one member, one vote (OMOV, as it became known). But the win was narrow, despite Smith's decision to resign as leader if his reform was not accepted.

The triumvirate of Tony Blair, Gordon Brown and Peter Mandelson was, ever so slowly, breaking up. The essential difference seemed to be that Blair and Mandelson were prepared to go far further in criticising and undermining John Smith than Brown wished to go. 'Mandelson was briefing that the three of them thought Smith was not modern enough or radical enough' says John Edmonds. 'John was worried about it, but he was indulgent towards Brown and Blair. He hated Mandelson.' Mandelson even struck a sour note about Smith's victory at the October conference, trying to force Smith to take a more antagonistic line towards the unions. 'We had a deal over OMOV' says John Edmonds. 'And it unravelled because Mandelson was determined that it should unravel.'

Having told Blair which job to take, Brown told him how to do it. Blair said he wanted to get rid of Labour's image as being soft on crime, and he thought of using the catchphrase 'tough on crime'. Brown advised him to add 'and tough on the causes of crime' because it would play better with Labour Party people. Blair followed the advice, though never quite seeming to understand the point of the amendment.

Blair launched it on the ITV programme *The World This Weekend* on 10 January 1993, and it did more than any other single thing to help him edge ahead of the man who had made it for him. At that year's party conference, for the first time ever, Tony Blair put his nose in front of his friend and mentor Gordon Brown: in elections for Labour's NEC, Blair came sixth and Brown came seventh.

Not, in 1993, that it seemed to matter much. Most people thought a Smith premiership could be no further away than 1997, and the battle for the succession would be fought in the new millennium. But early in the morning of 12 May 1994, John Smith had another heart attack. This time it killed him.

7

Deal or No Deal?

The few days after John Smith's death, ending with the moment when Gordon Brown stood down in favour of Tony Blair in Labour's leadership election, are among the most written about days in recent British political history. Meetings, at the Granita restaurant and elsewhere, have been remorselessly analysed, and if you have a mind to it, anything you want to know is in one of the many books, right down to what was eaten and how much was left on everyone's plate. (Gordon Brown, apparently, wasn't very hungry that famous night at the Granita, and who can blame him?)

Most of the literature is aimed at answering the question: was there, or was there not, a deal about the leadership – a clear understanding that, if Gordon Brown stepped aside and gave Tony Blair a clear run at the leadership, Blair would step down after a certain period of time, and let Brown take over?

Is Brown reading too much into some vague assurance from Blair that he would not go on forever? No, says former union leader John Edmonds, a confidante of Brown's in those days of opposition, there really was a deal: 'The deal was that after two periods of office, Tony Blair would step down and recommend Brown.'

It's not credible, says Neil Kinnock. 'I've never believed in it. I've never asked them but here are two young guys in 1994 who have only ever known opposition. Both were less certain than I was that we were going to win the next general election. They would not be sitting there making this sort of deal, it would have been castles in the air. Neither of them would have found the arrogance to make a deal on the carving up of power.'

I doubt whether there will ever be a definitive answer. Brownites say there was, and Blairites say there wasn't, and there's an end to it.

Fortunately, I consider this an uninteresting question, at least for my present purpose, which is to understand Gordon Brown. The interesting question is: why did Brown step aside? Even if there was a deal, he was handing over to someone else the prize of his lifetime.

And Brown is a historian. He knows that Prime Ministers never leave the job voluntarily, whatever they say or think before they start it. It's addictive. Every Prime Minister has to be dragged out of Downing Street, kicking and screaming. The only one to have left voluntarily in the 20th century was Harold Wilson, who (to his everlasting credit) recognised the first signs of a terrible illness. Even had there been a deal, Brown must have known that it might not be honoured. He knows too that Harold Wilson was right: a week really is a long time in politics, and a few years is a lifetime. Brown could not guarantee that, at a given time in the future, he would still be the front-runner.

Anyway, what was wrong with a contest, in which one of the front-runners would be defeated? That, after all, is the way Labour has always elected its leader. Kinnock was elected that way in 1983, and his opponent Roy Hattersley became his loyal deputy. Foot was elected in 1980 and his rival Dennis Healey served as his deputy. In 1976 Callaghan defeated Foot, in 1963 Wilson defeated George Brown – never before had an obvious front-runner felt unable to compete for the job. So why should Brown feel that in 1994?

What was Brown thinking? If we can establish that, we will learn a lot about him. But it isn't a simple question.

Let's start with the two most hostile interpretations, both Blairite, but mutually contradictory. Charles Clarke, one of the earliest and most loyal of the Blairites, is on record as saying that he wishes Brown had stood, and been soundly defeated, as Clarke is sure he would have been. Clarke thinks Brown's decision was a calculation. He could not win, therefore his best course was to extract everything he could from the situation, and he extracted from Blair more than he was entitled to. The other hostile Blairite view is exactly the opposite: that Brown failed at the crucial moment, as he will always fail at crucial moments, because he lacks that decisiveness and self-belief without which you cannot do the top job – just as he had failed to challenge John Smith in 1992. It is this view that lies at the root of Charles Clarke's unexpected verdict, that Brown has 'psychological flaws'.

From one extreme to the other, here is what the arch Brownite Nick Brown told me. Nick Brown is short, stout, quiet-spoken and affable, with the political cunning he learned as an official for the GMB trade union before he was elected MP for Newcastle upon Tyne East and Wallsend in 1983. Nick Brown organised the campaigns which saw both Gordon Brown and Blair rocketed into the Shadow Cabinet. By 1994 he was in the Gordon Brown camp, and the day John Smith died, he was clear that they could win – if his man declared quickly. To stand any chance, Gordon needed to make his candidature clear on the day of Smith's death, and allow his friends to canvass support. *decisive*

Smith died at 9.15 a.m. and by 4 p.m. (and probably earlier) Blair was telling his friends that he was going to stand, come what may. That was when his friend John Carr reached him on the telephone to say: 'Don't let them talk you into letting Gordon be the candidate', and Blair replied: 'Don't worry. They won't.'

From Gordon's side, Nick Brown confirms the speed. 'Alun Michael and Peter Kilfoyle were getting people lined up for Blair from the start, and Gordon would not let us do the same for him. If he had said he was going to run, we could have got him the nominations and then we could have won.' But they would have had to move very fast. By the time Brown actually withdrew, he had no choice. The Blair campaign was so advanced that he might have struggled just to get the required number of nominations, says Nick Brown.

For this, Nick Brown points out, was what made the 1994 leadership contest different from previous ones. The number of nominations required to stand had been raised to 12.5 per cent of the Parliamentary Labour Party, so as to prevent anyone doing to the leader what Tony Benn had done to Neil Kinnock, and standing against him without a chance of winning, in order to provide a platform. 'My calculation was that by the time Gordon withdrew, we had fallen below the number we needed to get him nominated,' says Nick Brown.

So Gordon Brown knew he had to move fast, and knew that Blair was moving fast. Letting the moment pass was, effectively, to rule himself out. All the meetings, secret assignations in the Edinburgh home of a friend of Blair's and in Blair's constituency, in Granita and other London restaurants, all relentlessly catalogued in the voluminous literature, the deals, the negotiations, the written agreement – they were just dancing minuets round each other. The decision was made in that first 24 hours, if not even faster than that, when Brown refused to let his friends start campaigning.

By the time John Smith was buried, though no one knew it, Gordon Brown's decision was made. 'I told him at John Smith's funeral that he should stand,' says the economic journalist William Keegan. 'And I could sense that I'd said the wrong thing.' Right from the start, at some level, Brown knew he was going to stand aside for Blair. Why?

Nick Brown says that starting as fast as Blair would have outraged Gordon's sense of decorum. Paul Routledge writes that against the conspiratorial backdrop created by the Blair camp, 'Brown was behaving more like a grieving friend than an ambitious politician.' Charlie Whelan, who had recently started working for Brown on media relations, told Routledge: 'He only seemed interested in writing obituaries. We spent the whole day doing that. He didn't feel up to doing any interviews. Everybody was asking "Where's Gordon Brown?" … We didn't have any clue while this was going on that people were plotting for the leadership.'[1]

This is not entirely convincing. Perhaps Whelan did not know what was going on, but Nick Brown did. And Gordon Brown may be decorous and gentlemanly, but he is also a successful professional politician, and professional politicians know you have to do indecorous things sometimes. He knew what was going on. He walked away with his eyes open.

But Nick Brown also has a more convincing explanation to offer. 'We could have won. But we would have done so much damage to the modernising cause. There was a danger we would have to summon up awful forces to win.' The Brown campaign would have had to paint Blair as the ultra right-winger in order to win, he says.

It is certainly true that, if Brown had fought, he would have had to mobilise the left against Blair, and would have had to paint Blair (accurately) as being on the far right of the Labour Party. Constituency activists would have had to be mobilised to pressurise MPs, as they had been by the Bennites in the bad old days.

The left might afterwards have felt betrayed. But that, too, is something that happens in politics. Harold Wilson was the left-wing candidate, the old Bevanite who proved rather more pragmatic in leadership than his supporters would have wished. Having to paint your opponent black does not stop professional politicians from running for the top job. We are not quite there.

Neil Kinnock told me that he was keen for them not to run against each other: 'There were too many memories of Labour as a divided party on journalists' computers which will produce "Labour split". Maybe it was me being ultra cautious but it was a factor in their minds, as became clear. I said to them both, together and separately, you are the people who decide who the candidate is, don't let anyone do it for you.' If they did both run, 'the result would have been 53–47. The ultra caution in me said it was better not to be a 50/50 race. But if it had been, it would have had to be managed, and it would have been managed.'

I pointed out to Kinnock that he and Hattersley had run against each other and the sky did not fall in – in fact they worked well together as leader and deputy. He said: 'That says a lot about Roy, and it might even say something about me.' So perhaps he did not quite trust Brown and Blair to behave as well as he and Hattersley had behaved – though he did add, after a moment: 'I'm sure it could have been done in 1994, it would have been manageable.'

Which did Kinnock want? 'I had no preference' he said, then added: 'After 1992, circumstances changed conditions negatively to Gordon, positively to Tony. I was aware that Gordon as Shadow Chancellor had depressed expectations and refused to let people make spending commitments. He was known as the abominable no-man.' Actually, Kinnock the inveterate phrase-maker invented the name 'the abominable no-man'. He'll even own up to it if you press him. Somewhere beneath the careful statesmanlike phrases, the ginger-haired political imp still lurks.

'I was also aware,' Kinnock told me, 'that Tony was performing very well in the Home Office brief. The only other consideration that was relevant to me was that Tony was married with kids and Gordon had yet to settle down, despite a stream of terrific girlfriends, some of whom I knew.' It is odd that even now, people feel it necessary to point to Brown's girlfriends, as though being unmarried for all those years raises a question mark which he has not quite got rid of. At the time, Blairite MPs, still believing Brown might run, were phoning waverers and saying: 'Do you really think we need another Scot, and one who's unmarried, for leader?'[2] Two years later, Sue Lawley said to him on *Desert Island Discs*: 'It is something that middle-aged men and women have to put up with: people want to know whether you're gay or whether there's some flaw in your personality that you haven't made a relationship.' By then, Brown's stream of girlfriends was pretty well known.

Kinnock was not alone in seeing the two men's domestic arrangements as an issue. Tony Blair was a conventional young-vergingon-middle-aged man, with a lawyer wife, children, an attractive and tastefully furnished home in Islington. Kinnock the devoted family man understood the Blairs, and more importantly, he knew that the middle-class voters in the south east whom Labour needed would understand the Blairs.

Brown was a known workaholic with little interest in clothes or in his surroundings. He had bought an attractive home in Edinburgh but taken no trouble with furnishing or decorating it, and it was always littered with his papers. He bought his dark suits and red ties in bulk to save time. It was said that he possessed no clothes for relaxing in, since he never relaxed. When I put this to his friends, they first assure me it is not true, then try hard to remember him in relaxation mode. Kinnock thought for a while, then said: 'I've never been to a rugby game with him when he hasn't worn a suit. I think I saw him wearing a sports coat once, many years ago, Harris Tweed number it was, and I think he has some pullovers. It's always my image of Gordon, with a white shirt.'

It was not an accident that after Neil Kinnock's resignation as Labour leader, pink ties started appearing around the neck of the Shadow Chancellor, though today they have mostly been displaced by the old red ones. Kinnock's assistant Sue Nye went to work for Brown. Kinnock told me the story. 'Sue Nye said, you've got to do something about your ties, and he said, OK, get me a tie, so she makes sure there's a supply of them. Gordon's a big, good looking guy, girls used to really fancy him, but nothing will ever make him check the mirror before he goes out because it's the last thing on his mind. If you say, shouldn't you brush your shoulders, he'd say why?' Kinnock finds this strange. 'I couldn't go out without my shoes shined, a crease in my trousers, I'd hear my father saying, you polish those, a little trouble doesn't cost anything.' One of Brown's former girlfriends, Carol Craig, says: 'He is the sort of man that you feel you would have to take to have a haircut or get the right shoes.'[3]

A man who does not want to spend his days inspecting clothes, curtains and bathroom fittings seems a very strange creature to British voters, who value a conventional lifestyle above most other things. Or, if voters do not think that, politicians and their spin doctors believe they do, which is why – as Robin Cook used to point out with irritation – the House of Commons is the last workplace in the land where a dark suit is an everyday requirement. British society, much more than it did 20 years ago, demands conformity. It thinks that men (or women) in their forties without partners and children are a strange breed, not entirely to be trusted.

Add to that the fact that most of the seats Labour needed to win were in England, and were thought less likely to vote for a Scot, and you have something to add to the mix of motives in Brown's mind: a fear that no risk must be taken with the next election, and the man with the most conventional lifestyle must lead the party into it. Brown also understood another problem. If you accepted that Labour, in order to win, had to change further and faster than John Smith was changing it, then you accepted that the party needed Tony Blair. However, Blair and Peter Mandelson had also spent the year before John Smith's death undermining him.

Mandelson had an obvious reason. Smith didn't trust him and couldn't stand him, and from a position of great influence under Kinnock, he found himself with none. Blair was certain that Labour needed constant revolution. He believed that without frantic change, Labour would still lose. If you thought that, even now after four defeats in a row, Labour might be denied the prize, then Blair was your man.

Some Labour people were wondering if they would ever form a government again. Kinnock had no doubts – he was sure the next election would be won, as John Smith had been. But Blair and Brown both doubted. Kinnock thinks that 'if five or six of the big trade unions had said, it's Gordon Brown for us, then the arithmetic would have changed the chemistry. But that wasn't going to be the case. There was an extraordinary swirl in the party at the time. It was only two years since we had lost, there were feelings of fragility.'

If John Smith had died a year earlier, or even a year later, he would probably have been succeeded by Gordon Brown, not by Tony Blair. But in the end, in 1994 I think Brown doubted victory enough to stand aside, because he knew for certain – as Kinnock did not until many years later – that Tony Blair was not going to stand aside.

Once he was ready to tell people, there were a lot of friends and supporters to telephone, and Brown did not hand the job to anyone else. He spent the evening and the next morning on the phone. These must have been among the most dispiriting few hours of his life. 'Very early in the morning there was a call on my private line from Gordon Brown' says John Edmonds, then leader of the important GMB trade union. 'He said: "I'm not going to stand." I asked some questions, but he didn't answer them, he just restated the position. I said, I'm really very sorry. He said he had to phone a lot of people that morning.'

Edmonds meant it. He really was sorry. By then he was clear in his mind about the difference between Blair and Brown. He knew Blair had spoken of his impatience with John Smith, and Brown had not. At the previous year's Labour Party conference, he had seen Peter Mandelson, with Blair's support, briefing against Smith, undermining the deal which Edmonds and Smith had done, and demanding that Smith should 'stand up to' the unions. 'In all this, Gordon Brown was suddenly much quieter than Tony Blair,' he says. 'Blair and Mandelson were destabilising John Smith's leadership.'

Brown was convinced, first, that Blair was more certain of being able to deliver victory at the next election than he was; and second, that a battle between them would end with the victor, whoever it was, tarnished right up to the time of the election. By the time the contest was over, Brown would have painted Blair as an extreme and cynical right-winger who would do nothing for the poor, and Blair would have painted Brown as a Neanderthal relic of Labour's tax-and-spend past.

If it was not right, it was not right. The psychology of Brown's decision-making again, at the most critical moment of all. Just as he would not fight for the parliamentary nomination in Hamilton in his mid-twenties, just as he would not take Kinnock's offer of a front bench job when new to parliament, he would not fight Blair for the leadership in 1994. I think Brown knew on the day of John Smith's death, or at least by the end of the following day, that he was not going to run.

8

The New Chancellor

Right up to the day of his general election victory in 1997, Tony Blair did not quite believe in it. He certainly never dreamed of a majority of 179. Blair had taken no chances. He dramatically persuaded Labour to abandon Clause Four, which committed the party to nationalisation. He re-christened his party New Labour, and stamped on anything which might look like old Labour squeeze-the-rich thinking. When education spokesman David Blunkett was quoted one morning suggesting Labour might charge VAT on private school fees, Blair's abrupt rebuke arrived in plenty of time for Blunkett to eat his words on that day's *The World at One* on Radio 4.

His Shadow Chancellor used language seldom heard before in Labour Party circles. Brown's first big speech of 1995 was entitled *The Dynamic Market Economy*. 'Wholesale nationalisation is not the way to ensure an economy run in the public interest,' he said. The only renationalisation he would commit himself to was the railways – the one privatisation of the Major government, and one which most observers believe was a dreadfully botched job which had done huge damage.

Brown moved the party away from the idea of universal benefits, obtainable as a right of citizenship, towards targeting – the means-testing which Labour had once hated. And he promised a referendum before Britain entered the European Monetary Union.

He even outflanked the Tories on tax, promising a starting rate of 15 pence in the pound, moving to 10 pence when it could be afforded; no increase in the top rate of tax, which the Conservatives had brought down from 83 to 40 pence in the pound; and no new commitments which required additional spending. The only exception to this was a welfare-to-work programme to be funded by a windfall tax on privatised utilities.

Brown promised there would be no spending commitments requiring new taxation, which is why so few of the pledges in the 1997 manifesto cost money. One exception was reducing class sizes in schools – but only because it was to be financed by a cut in the same department, namely getting rid of the assisted places scheme. No wonder his old Edinburgh enemy Robin Cook and his newer but equally fierce enemy, the deputy leader John Prescott, tried to have him reined in, and to prevent him wandering at will into every other department's business.

There is room for doubt as to whether all this was necessary. Did Labour need to tie its own hands so tightly for its first five years in government? Brown, and more particularly Blair, mistakenly thought the election dreadfully finely balanced (an estimate with which their old boss Neil Kinnock disagreed – he was confident of their victory). Labour's troubles had been more about disunity than policy, and Labour was now relatively united, while the Conservatives were so split over Europe that in the last years in power their government could hardly function. At one point John Major even resigned as Conservative Leader, challenging his Eurosceptic opponents to put up or shut up. He won his job back, but they did not shut up.

While the Conservatives were fatally disunited, Labour had managed to put its days of internecine feuding behind it. Neil Kinnock and John Smith had bequeathed Tony Blair a relatively united party. The new division – the Blair/Brown feud – was in the future. The old Blair/Brown friendship was more or less dead after the events of May 1994, but a business partnership developed, born out of the fact that they agreed broadly about what needed to be done; and they were yoked together.

In those three years of opposition, Blair and Brown only disagreed, as far as we know, on two matters, but those two are significant for what they tell us about the difference between the two men. Brown would have liked to propose raising the top rate of tax to 50 pence, but Blair vetoed it. Blair would have liked to promise to find £60 million to replace the Royal Yacht *Britannia*, but Brown said no without asking Blair. Even these were kept secret. They were so pessimistic about the election that they believed they could not afford to allow a sliver of public disagreement between them to show.

Brown's cautious doubt about the result was not dispelled until lunchtime on polling day, 1 May 1997, when his press officer, Charlie Whelan, gave him the interim results of the BBC's exit poll. Unless an election is desperately close, the BBC's exit poll is accurate quite early in the day.

At lunchtime Brown spoke from his Edinburgh home to Blair, at home in Sedgefield. There was a foretaste of future trouble: Blair unsuccessfully tried to persuade Brown not to take his whole inner cabinet – Ed Balls, Sue Nye, Charlie Whelan and Ed Miliband – into government with him. Then Brown flew to London, attended the official celebration at the Festival Hall on the South Bank, and went to a penthouse flat at the Grosvenor House Hotel overlooking Hyde Park owned by his multi-millionaire MP friend Geoffrey Robinson, where he slept for a couple of hours before starting life in government.

His four key staff were with him when he walked into the Treasury at 4 p.m. the next afternoon. As he climbed the elegant staircase, his civil servants burst into applause, which surprised and delighted the new Chancellor. Permanent Secretary Sir Terence Burns showed them into the Chancellor's office and tried to start a briefing, but Brown cut him off and handed him an envelope, while Balls, Nye,

Whelan and Miliband discreetly left them alone. They knew that the letter contained dynamite. Burns's jaw dropped as he read it.[1] It was a letter to Eddie George, Governor of the Bank of England, telling him the Chancellor wished to hand over the power to set interest rates to the Bank – a dramatic shift in monetary policy.

It had huge symbolic as well as practical importance. The fall of the second Labour government in 1931 was caused by a financial crisis, exacerbated by the Gold Standard. Labour was replaced by a National Government – effectively a Conservative government – which promptly left the Gold Standard. 'No one told us we could do that,' complained Sidney Webb, who had founded the Fabian Society and was in the 1929–31 government.

The result was that Labour felt betrayed by the Bank of England, and the party cheered when the next Labour Chancellor, Hugh Dalton, nationalised it immediately after the 1945 election. Was Brown reversing Dalton's decision? Partly – enough to assure the City that the new Chancellor was really on their side. Interest rates would in future be decided, not by the Chancellor, but by a new Monetary Policy Committee over which the Bank's Governor would preside. But the Chancellor continued to appoint its members and set inflation targets. He had not given away as much of the power Hugh Dalton had taken as he liked to make it appear.

On his US visits, Brown had noticed that interest rates never became a political issue, as they did in Britain, and was impressed by the arguments for an independent central bank after the US model. But it was only in the last few days of the election campaign that he decided to make it the first thing he did. It meant making his staff and his civil servants work through the weekend. By Monday, the May Bank Holiday, he was ready to tell the Governor of his new powers, and Eddie George was sent for.

The secret, amazingly, was kept until the planned announcement the next day, and it was the best possible start for the new government – bold, dramatic, unexpected, and, when they got used to the idea, considered brilliant by experts on all sides.

The next big thing was less of a surprise, though civil servants did not expect it to arrive so well worked out. It was the Windfall Tax – the only way of getting some money which Brown and Blair had not closed down for fear of frightening Middle England. Utility companies which had profited enormously from privatisation under the Conservatives were to have some of their largesse prised away from them as a one-off levy. And with the money, Brown was going to do something concrete about youth unemployment. But it had to be lawyer-proof. The utility companies had plenty of money to spend on the very best lawyers. The key was working out which utilities would pay, and how much.

So, before the election, in the greatest secrecy, Ed Balls and Geoffrey Robinson recruited and consulted the best lawyers and accountants they could find. They all had to have some other excuse for working on the idea, in case Brown had to deny that he knew what they were doing. He refused to give even Sir Terence Burns the details. The careful preparation paid dividends. BT Chairman Sir Iain Vallance attacked the Windfall Tax and said he would challenge it in the courts, soon after announcing profits which amounted to £100 every second. Brown said nothing. In his desk he had a letter from Vallance saying that he recognised Labour had won a mandate for the tax. He mentioned the matter quietly, and no more was heard from Sir Iain.

Apart from the Windfall Tax, the only other additional sum available to satisfy the inevitable demands for money from health and education was £2.2 billion from the contingency reserve, the money the Treasury set aside for a rainy day, which Brown secretly decided to use in his first budget.

Eddie George's triumph was short-lived. He quickly found that Brown intended also to strip the Bank of England of its role as city regulator, and to beef up the Securities and Investment Board to take on the role. The Bank did not have a good record as city policeman in recent years, having failed to prevent some high-profile collapses, such as the Middle East-controlled BCCI, which went down in 1991. But Eddie George was not going to be pleased, especially since he thought he had an assurance from Brown that such a step would not be taken without further consultation. When he went back to the Treasury two weeks later and Brown broke it to him, he was furious. He admitted to a press conference that he briefly considered resignation, which would have shaken City confidence disastrously, so near the start of Brown's watch. He didn't do it, the storm passed, and Brown was able to boast the legacy of a stronger regulatory regime.

Eddie George did not find his new boss as easy to get on with as his previous one. As Hugh Pym and Nick Kochan explain, it had a lot to do with their contrasting personalities: 'Ken Clarke and Eddie George may have fallen out over interest rate policy but they could always enjoy a drink together afterwards. Both had the outgoing cheeriness of regulars in a saloon bar ... Brown and George were from different moulds and in a year of such upheaval it was hardly surprising that working relationships should be frayed.'

Brown and Ed Balls associated Eddie George with past failures they hoped to avoid, especially an excessive devotion to fighting inflation, and they also hoped, without much evidence, that he would resign, or at least have no wish for reappointment when his term of office ran out on 30 June 1998. One of their list of possible governors was the economist Gavyn Davies of Goldman Sachs, who is married to Sue Nye. However, the City rallied round George, especially after a Labour spin doctor said he had 'played into our hands' with his remarks about the European single currency. Tony Blair supported George, too, especially after he found that the City supported him.[2] He was reappointed for another five years.

Brown's relationship with Eddie George recovered. They put aside their differences and discovered, if not exactly affection, at least professional respect for each other. There was no such happy ending with his Permanent Secretary, Sir Terence Burns, who felt his new boss had not been straight with him at first. Burns left after a year, in June 1998, and was succeeded by Sir Andrew Turnbull, who stayed with Brown until he was appointed Cabinet Secretary in 1992. Eddie George retired that year, and Brown delivered a sincere tribute to him at the Mansion House dinner.

There was more, much more, in a whirlwind few months. As expected, the government signed up to the European Social Chapter and ended the ban on trade unions at the GCHQ spy headquarters. When the cabinet met on 8 May, ministers were instructed to follow the example set by Prime Minister and Chancellor, and forgo until the following April the £16,000-a-year pay rises which had been agreed. The Queen's Speech two days later promised a national minimum wage.

There was also the Millennium Dome to deal with. This was a vast structure to be built at Greenwich to celebrate the Millennium, planned by the outgoing Conservative government; but no one had thought of anything to go in the thing. There is plenty of evidence that Brown wanted to scrap it – a course which we now know would have saved the nation both huge expense and huge embarrassment.

Brown went about his mission crabwise. At the Cabinet on 20 June, when the issue was still in the balance, Brown unexpectedly produced 'five tests' for the Dome before it could go ahead – a precursor of his famous five tests for whether Britain joined the Euro. These included a demand that the exhibition would be permanent – at a stroke putting up the cost by £15 million – as the site could not be sold. No new public money should go into the project, and the targets of £175 million business sponsorship and £136 million ticket sales must be reached. The content must be more exciting, must relate to the whole nation, and a new management structure must 'provide ideas and a creative force'.

But Brown was dealing with a Prime Minister who was determined to go ahead with the project, and the Prime Minister won. It is interesting to examine how he went about it, for it was a sort of dry run for future disagreements. Brown's five tests were leaked to newspapers – but as Blair's tests, not Brown's tests. Meanwhile Blair's cabinet allies were assembled. John Prescott suddenly remembered how he enjoyed his childhood visit to the 1951 Festival of Britain, and Peter Mandelson recalled affectingly how his grandfather had been behind that venture.

Blair had to leave cabinet early, and left his deputy John Prescott with instructions not to take a vote. If a vote had been taken, the project would have been killed, there and then, as furious spending ministers – Health Secretary Frank Dobson, Education Secretary David Blunkett – demanded to know why the money could not be put to good use in their departments. Blair went to the Greenwich site and told the world that the project was going ahead. And that was that. There was no going back. Brown's five tests were quietly forgotten.[3]

Despite this defeat, the new Chancellor had hit Whitehall like a whirlwind. His working day began in his office at 7.30 in the morning, and he would get back to his flat in time to watch *Newsnight* on BBC2 at 10.30 p.m. He showed little respect for established ways of doing things, or for tradition. When he spoke at the annual Mansion House dinner on 12 June, he caused a flutter by refusing to wear the traditional tails, or at least dinner jacket. He wore one of those dark suits he bought in bulk. You have to look back to the 1940s for a precedent. Aneurin Bevan was the despair of his Prime Minister, Clement Attlee, for his refusal to wear a dinner jacket at formal events. Bevan said it was because a dinner jacket was the uniform of the ruling class, but Brown was studiously avoiding that sort of language, so it is not clear what this act of rebellion was about. By the time Brown set off for his month-long summer holiday in Cape Cod, he felt content that he had – in the management-speak employed by Charlie Whelan – hit the ground running.

9

Brown and the Brownites

With Gordon Brown in Cape Cod that summer was Sarah Macaulay. He had entered government with a new woman in his life, and this time it was permanent.

At the start of the 1990s he had taken up with an old flame from STV days, journalist Sheena Macdonald, now working for the BBC in London. After he met Sarah Macaulay in early 1994, just before John Smith's death, he seems to have dumped Macdonald with an abruptness that was almost brutal. He met the woman he was to marry when he was 43, married her in 2000 six years later when he was pushing 50, and was nearly 51 when his first child was born. It was, you might think, a bit late, though a group of his old friends, including Wilf Stevenson, were getting married at the same sort of age about that time. I think there are three factors at work here.

First, like many of the Sixties generation, he never thought of himself as anything other than a young man. Second, he was always too busy – several former relationships had foundered on the fact that he would not find time and space in his life for them, and they had to come a bad fourth to politics, politics and politics. There was always an important meeting, phone call, or piece of work to finish, and perhaps they took precedence over taking the time needed to get to know, understand and love another human being.

But the third factor is something so central to Gordon Brown's psychology that it is worth dwelling on for a moment. Brown is a man who will wait as long as it takes, whatever the objective happens to be and however much he wants it; and he will not hurry. Hurrying, he believes, will not necessarily deliver. He is the ultimate long gamer. Getting into Parliament? The early chance he might have had didn't suit his personal circumstances, and it didn't feel right. Getting onto the Shadow Cabinet? He had an offer at an early age, when most young politicians would jump at it, but it didn't feel right. Getting to be Labour leader? He would have liked the job earlier than he is going to have it, but fighting for it in 1994 was not quite right, given the media and other pressures of the time. Many politicians in his position would have fought, fearing that their chance would slip away. Brown chose to wait, to play the long game, to back his own judgement on the right timing. But he never for one moment lost sight of the objective.

It seems to me – though at least one friend of Brown's strongly disagrees with me – that it was also like that in his relationships with women. The occasional glimpses of his personal life which he allowed to interviewers show that he always wanted to get married. But it never felt quite right, until Sarah.

There is one other factor to put into the mix. When I told Dianne Abbott, the left-wing Labour MP for Hackney North and Stoke Newington, that I was writing a biography of Gordon Brown, I expected to hear some pretty harsh comments. What she said, with evident affection, was: 'He's a very, very shy man.' His mother Elizabeth Brown watched his political rise with bewilderment. 'I am amazed that he does this.' she told Paul Routledge. 'He was the shyest member of the family when he was very young. The other boys were extroverts, but Gordon was the opposite.' And she is talking of a time before the dreadful months in his late teens when he thought he was going to go blind. Wilf Stevenson does not consider his friend to be shy. 'He has a firm sense of privacy, and a wish to separate public from private life,' he says. 'When you see him in his constituency, and how ready people are to approach him and just chat with him, you get a better sense of his inner being.'

Nevertheless, it seems to me that there is something in him that has made it hard for him to suggest to a woman that she should spend the rest of her life with him and have his children. Yet he seems to have known, sometime between 1994 and 1997, that he had finally met the woman he was going to marry.

One frequently-touted explanation can be ruled out. Cynics say the events of 1994 showed Brown that if he hoped ever to be Prime Minister, he should get married, so he did. But if his motives were cynically political, he would surely have asked Sarah to marry him before the 1997 election. This, among other things, would have saved Charlie Whelan a problem. The tradition was that the Chancellor posed with his wife, and Whelan did not want Brown posing alone for his first budget – it would revive comment about his unmarried state. So he arranged for Brown to have with him a group of apprentices from Rosyth, and told his boss that no matter how much the photographers shouted 'One on your own, sir' he must not move away from the apprentices. Just one newspaper cheated, and digitally manipulated the picture to remove the apprentices – surprisingly, it was *The Guardian*.

Sarah Macaulay's mother was a teacher and her father worked for publishers Longman. She was born in October 1963. Her parents separated when she was seven, and she lived with her mother and her two younger brothers in north London, going to school, first at Acland Burghley comprehensive, then (for the sixth form) to the prestige comprehensive, Camden School for Girls. She was one of the ringleaders of a clique known as 'the Trendies', famed for stunts such as spraying themselves in gold body paint for a party.

After a psychology degree at Bristol University, she started work with PR agency Wolff Olins writing annual reports and brochures – the dogsbody end of public relations. She wanted more, and wanted it quickly. In 1988, aged only 25, she and three friends formed their own design agency, Spirit Design, to provide companies with corporate images. It was the essence of Thatcher's Britain: four bright young people selling logos and branding. And it did what bright young companies did in the Eighties: made money fast, then went bust in 1994.

Undeterred, she went into partnership with her old schoolfriend Julia Hobsbawm, daughter of the famous Communist historian Eric Hobsbawm. Their PR firm, Hobsbawm Macaulay, quickly landed contracts with causes close to Labour, including the *New Statesman*, owned by Geoffrey Robinson, a Brown ally. These brought her into contact with key people round Brown – Sue Nye, Charlie Whelan – and she met Brown briefly at Labour events. In the spring of 1994, when the two shared a flight from London to Scotland for the Scottish Labour party conference just before John Smith's death, they got to know each other better.

For years, Brown refused to talk about the relationship, and though journalists wrote about it, the romance was not made public until 1997, when Whelan staged a photo opportunity in London restaurant Vasco & Piero's. Even then Brown wanted deniability – the *News of the World* photographer was told to make it look as though he had 'snatched' the carefully posed picture. It had to be reshot when Brown failed to look suitably loving.

By then Sarah certainly knew the worst. No girlfriend, and probably no wife, was ever going to supplant the office in Brown's affections. The key people in his life in 1997, after his two brothers Andrew and John, were his four principal aides, one or two key friends and advisers, and his immediate political deputies at the Treasury. To understand Brown we need to know something about them.

Brown is most comfortable with people he has known for a long time. The Browns are a very close family and the two people closest to the Chancellor, to whose advice he will always listen, are his elder brother John, public relations executive for Glasgow City Council and editor of the council's newspaper, and his younger brother Andrew, a television producer until, in 2003, he went to work for Weber Shandwick, the public relations company headed by the former Labour Party chief press officer Colin Byrne. Ironically, Byrne is a Blairite through and through, and one of those who worked to frustrate Gordon Brown's leadership hopes in 1994.

Next to them come two old friends whose advice Brown always seeks when it is available. The oldest friend he has is Murray Elder, whom he met before he was five. They went together from primary school to Kirkcaldy High School. Both were selected for the experiment which rocketed them ahead of their peers, and had them taking A-levels and going to university when they were just 16. Elder was John Smith's political adviser during the 1979–83 Parliament, and even then seemed to be older and wiser than the other youthful Shadow Cabinet advisers. He was general secretary of the Scottish Labour Party between 1988 and 1992. He might well have become a major political figure in his own right were it not for serious heart problems.

Wilf Stevenson, four years older than Brown, was research officer for Edinburgh University Student Union from 1970–4, when Brown was a key figure, becoming Rector in 1972. Ever since then, he has been a key friend and adviser, and is likely to move into Downing Street when Brown becomes Prime Minister. Stevenson was educated at a minor Scottish public school, the Edinburgh Academy, and University College, Oxford. He was director of the British Film Institute for 10 years, 1988–98, and left to run the Smith Institute, a think-tank set up in memory of the late John Smith which is considered to be the cradle of the thinking which is to inform a Brown premiership.

The Smith Institute's closeness to the Chancellor cannot be overestimated. It shares an office with the *New Statesman*, which was bought by Brown's millionaire ally Geoffrey Robinson with the intention of using it, when the time came, to ensure that the Labour Party elected Brown to lead it. Robinson pays the Institute's office rent. When the *New Statesman* appoints a new editor or political editor, Wilf Stevenson is one of those on the interview panel, and he is on the magazine's board. Robinson brought the *New Statesman* back into profitability partly by getting companies to sponsor supplements, and some companies believe that to do so will help them get access to Brown. As I write, the Smith Institute is being investigated by the Charity Commission for holding meetings at Number 11 Downing Street, whose purpose, it is alleged, strays into the political.

It was the Smith Institute that employed the Chancellor's key adviser Ed Balls for the few months that it might have been awkward for Brown to employ him. Balls was an adviser to Brown as Shadow Chancellor from 1994 to 1997, and went with him to the Treasury until 2004. But when he was adopted as a parliamentary candidate, it was diplomatic for him not to work for Brown, so he worked at the Smith Institute as a research fellow until he was elected MP for Normanton in 2005 and could move back to the Treasury the following year, this time as Economic Secretary. Balls was a youthful high flyer. After reading PPE at Keble College, Oxford, he taught at Harvard University (with which Brown has strong links – he works there whenever he is in the USA) before four years as a leader writer on the *Financial Times*. He met Brown in 1993, when both Blair and Brown were courting journalists they thought would be useful to them. The next year, still only 27 years old, he went to work for and advise Brown, and one way or another he has done so ever since.

Ed Miliband, who also joined Brown in 1994, is even younger than Ed Balls – he was 25 at the time. His father Ralph Miliband, one of the most significant and influential socialist historians and political thinkers of his generation, died the same year, and Gordon Brown of all people must have realised the significance of taking advice from Ralph Miliband's son, for Brown's PhD thesis is full of references to Ralph Miliband's work. Not that Miliband père would have appreciated the compliment. He believed the Labour Party had already made far too many compromises with capitalism, even before Brown and Blair came along. Ed Miliband and his older brother David, also an influential Labour MP, are careful not to get drawn into public discussions of their father.

Sue Nye, who organises Brown's diary and his life, worked for three Labour leaders in succession – James Callaghan, Michael Foot and Neil Kinnock. She was Kinnock's diary secretary, and controlled access to the leader so firmly that MPs who wanted to see him, or to get their constituency engagements into his diary, grew to resent her. When Kinnock resigned as leader in 1992, she went to work for Brown, and has been with him ever since. She is married to the millionaire banker, former BBC Chairman and Brown ally Gavyn Davies.

The oddest and most unexpected of the four key people around Brown in 1997 was his press officer, Charlie Whelan. A former public schoolboy who became a Communist in 1975 while studying politics at the City of London Polytechnic, Whelan spent ten years handling media relations for the Amalgamated Electrical and Engineering Union (AEEU.)

Big trade unions were in those days notoriously amateurish about their public relations, and in the small world of trade union press officers, Whelan did not stand out. He was a sociable, chain-smoking heavy drinker, able to keep his end up among hard-bitten hard-drinking union officials. He was loyal and had the discipline instilled by the Communist Party, of which he remained a member until 1990. AEEU boss Gavin Laird credited Whelan with a talent for getting Laird on television in preference to other union leaders. Crucially, Whelan got on well with the industrial correspondents, a group of journalists whom Tony Blair loathed because they drank hard in shabby pubs and sounded rather like the trade union officials they wrote about. Quite how this rather indiscreet, frequently profane, often careless and defiantly un-intellectual former Communist became the man whom the fastidious, workaholic, academic Brown was sure he needed is a mystery. But Whelan did, and he too joined the Shadow Chancellor's staff in 1994. As the unions declined, so did the industrial correspondents. Time was when they thought themselves an elite. Why would they want to hobnob with cabinet ministers when they were on fancy-a-pint terms with the general secretary of the Transport and General Workers Union? But as Whelan moved from the unions to politics, being an industrial correspondent was losing its appeal, and his old chums among the industrial correspondents started eyeing up lobby jobs hungrily. So in the lobby, Whelan found journalists he had dealt with for ten years, but who were new, strange and untrustworthy beasts to the spin doctors round Blair. 'Once an industrial correspondent, always an industrial correspondent' Peter Mandelson once said to one of those who made the change, the BBC's Nicholas Jones, and Mandelson did not mean it kindly.

So, as the lobby journalists started to divide themselves into Brownites and Blairites, it is no surprise that the former industrial correspondents, like Jones and the *Daily Mirror*'s Paul Routledge, tended to be in the Brown camp. They were one of Charlie Whelan's first gifts to his new boss. He and Paul Routledge started to have regular (and famously boozy) lunches together, becoming firm friends over the second (and sometimes the third) bottle of wine; and out of this friendship came Routledge's fine early biography of the new Chancellor.

Brown's ministerial team in those early days consisted of his fellow Scots Alastair Darling and Helen Liddell as well as Dawn Primarolo, but the key member was Geoffrey Robinson. Born in 1938, Robinson was 59 when he took office for the first time in 1997, and had a successful and controversial business and political career behind him. Starting as a researcher at Labour Party headquarters in 1964, he moved into business via Harold Wilson's Industrial Reorganisation Corporation, for which he helped to negotiate a loan for the motor company Leyland. After that, he went to work for Leyland in 1971, where his rise was meteoric. The next year, aged 33, he was running a small Italian car manufacturer Leyland had just bought, called Innocenti, which was making the successful Mini. Two years later, back in Britain, he ran Jaguar for Leyland, now renamed British Leyland (BL), where his left-wing credentials helped him to establish a relationship with the trade unions which had eluded his predecessors. This allowed him to increase production.

Unfortunately the rise in oil prices after 1973 meant that the market for luxury cars started to collapse.

Leaving BL in 1974 after a reorganisation he had opposed, he was elected MP for Coventry North West at a by-election the next year. He lobbied hard for government aid for the motorcycle manufacturer Meriden, and in 1978 became its chief executive. He was horrified by the appointment of Michael Edwardes to run BL with a brief to confront the unions and make wholesale redundancies. But this was 1979 and the dawn of Thatcherism. The Robinson policy of working with trade unions and using government subsidy to help industry was out of fashion. His business interests, and his relationship with a fabulously wealthy Belgian heiress called Joska Bourgeois, continued to make him wealthier during the Thatcher and Major years, while he grew close to Labour's rising stars Gordon Brown and Tony Blair. In those early days, both benefited from Robinson's largesse. The Blairs' first visit to Robinson's splendid Italian villa was in 1996. Brown has taken at least one of his various girlfriends for a romantic weekend at Robinson's almost equally splendid flat in Cannes.

After 1992, when the Blair and Brown camps began to separate, Robinson sided with Brown, who is, like Robinson, much more union-friendly than Blair. Robinson was disappointed that Blair and not Brown became leader in 1994. That same, year Joska Bourgeois died, leaving Robinson the main heir to her £35 million fortune, and two years later Robinson bought the *New Statesman* magazine and injected much needed capital into it. The undisclosed intention was that the magazine, which is traditionally influential in Labour circles, would be there to campaign for Brown whenever the moment came, though in the event its services were not used – much to the relief of Robinson's editors. Robinson bankrolls the Brown-supporting Smith Institute which shares the magazine's office.

Robinson's long wait for government office ended, like so many others, in 1997 when he became Paymaster in Gordon Brown's Treasury team. But he was not in government for long. *The Guardian* on 22 December 1998 carried a story that Peter Mandelson had lied about the sources of his finance for his £475,000 Notting Hill home in London. He had received an undisclosed £373,000 loan from Geoffrey Robinson, which he used to buy the house. Mandelson was Secretary of State at the Department of Trade and Industry and the department's inspectors were investigating Robinson over his links with the late disgraced tycoon Robert Maxwell. Mandelson had not told his Permanent Secretary or the Cabinet Secretary, Sir Richard Wilson, about the connection. Mandelson and Robinson were forced to resign. Blair later brought Mandelson back, but not Robinson. The ministerial career for which he had waited so long was over in not much more than a year. Though he remained an MP, Robinson started to work from the *New Statesman* magazine office, where he is based to this day.

10

Prudent to a Fault

Neil Kinnock wanted to be sure that I was making use of economic commentator William Keegan's book about Brown. 'Bill Keegan thinks Brown has been less progressive than he could have been' he said.

'Do you think Keegan's right?' I asked. There was a pause before the ever-loyal Kinnock said: 'No.' Then he said this, and I leave it to the reader to deconstruct it: 'I think he's been operating under the constraint of the need to perpetually demonstrate the responsibility, prudence, and practicality of the Labour approach, partly because he's a member of the government not the leader of the government.'

It takes a near-earthquake to get Kinnock to breathe a word of criticism of the Labour government. And when this master of the succinct and witty phrase starts churning out ready-made phrases like a cement mixer, it is normally a sign that he is not comfortable. As a young left-wing politician in the late 1970s, before he became leader, he was critical of the Callaghan government, but never used the language of betrayal, as many left-wingers did. He accused them of timidity. Since he was leader, he has been utterly loyal to his successors. He gets to see Gordon Brown about once a month, and Tony Blair a little less frequently, and can raise privately the things that trouble him. He considers that a great privilege, and thinks that to attack them in public would be an abuse of that privilege. Only on education, and only once, has he got out of his pram.

Keegan writes that Brown wanted above all things to prevent the label 'tax and spend' being stuck on the Labour Party again, as it had in the past. But all government is about tax and spend. The debate between left and right about "tax and spend" is essentially one of the degree to which governments should tax and spend. But this did not stop Gordon Brown and his colleagues from saying, for political and vote-catching purposes, that they were against the very concept of "tax and spend". This approach was a reaction, indeed an overreaction, not only to all those successive electoral defeats but also to the prevailing climate of the times.'

However, so powerful was Brown's fear of the 'tax and spend' label that he surprised his own officials with his moderation. In 1997, Treasury officials remembered that, 18 years earlier, they had felt unprepared for the scale of change which Margaret Thatcher's new Conservative government would demand. They were determined not to make the same mistake with Labour. But in the event, they anticipated more change than they got. Instead of the expected spending spree, the new Chancellor froze departmental spending for two years, ignoring the screams of the spending ministers, especially at Health and Education. He announced that he was going to stick to the Conservatives' spending plans. His Tory predecessor, Kenneth Clarke, has admitted that he would not have stuck to these plans, and Brown's officials did not expect him to either, but he did. 'We had the strength to take difficult decisions, including to freeze public spending for two years as we constructed a new monetary and fiscal regime' was how Brown described it in 2003, speaking to the Social Market Foundation at the Cass Business School in London.

It puzzled Treasury officials. Their new political masters had won a huge majority, at least in part because the voters wanted more money spent on health and education, and wanted it now. Every opinion poll, including Labour's own polling, confirmed that. Public services were suffering from decades of under-investment. Polling guru Bob Worcester of Mori had told John Smith, shortly before Smith died, that the public would put up with higher taxes if they knew the money was going on health and education, and Worcester believes Smith was going to horrify the Treasury by hypothecating taxes – levying taxes specifically designed for these purposes. But Brown was not going to do that. Brown and his Prime Minister seemed certain they had to spend the whole of Labour's first term demonstrating their financial orthodoxy, so as to earn the right to spend some money in their second term. So instead of being criticised for spending money, the government was attacked for allowing public services to continue to rot.

Surprised Treasury mandarins found that once Brown had raised the money from the Windfall Tax on the profits of privatised utilities to finance his Welfare to Work scheme, his appetite for spending money was almost sated. He did what little he could to raise money in ways he hoped would not be noticed – thus were born what the Conservatives gleefully called 'stealth taxes' – and he discreetly geared some personal tax changes towards helping the low paid, as well as providing a little money for health and education.

One of these means of raising money has come back to haunt Brown. He scrapped the tax credits which were paid to pension funds. Geoffrey Robinson explains: 'Andersens' initial calculations – which in the end turned out to be spot on – were that the abolition of tax credits would benefit the Exchequer to the extent of approximately £5 billion per annum on an ongoing basis. We needed the money. It had to come from somewhere. We anticipated a huge hullabaloo from all quarters. But if the target was going to be met then tax credits had to go.'[1]

According to Tony Blair's former economics adviser Derek Scott, Blair had doubts about it, fearing its effect on pension funds, and it is now being suggested that it is one of the causes of the present pensions crisis, and the closure of many employers' final salary pension schemes. Brown defends it by saying that his action helped economic growth, through creating extra investment and allowing reductions in corporation tax. At a Glasgow press conference during the 2007 local government elections, Brown said: 'If I were making the same decision again, this would be the right decision for Britain.' His declaration will be compared, wrote the *Daily Telegraph* hopefully, 'to that of Norman Lamont, the former Conservative Chancellor, who famously declared "*je ne regrette rien*" a year after Black Wednesday, in which Britain was embarrassingly forced out of the European Exchange Rate Mechanism.'[2] Brown might with justice have pointed out that, in 1997, many employers considered their staff pension funds so well endowed that they were taking 'pension fund holidays' – that is, not paying into them for a while. If employers thought their pension funds were so well off that they could do without the money, it's a bit rich for them now to complain that the Chancellor should have realised that this was untrue. But that is the sort of anti-business argument that Brown has schooled himself never to use.

In the whole of Labour's first term, 1997–2001, public spending grew more slowly than it had done under John Major. And each year that Labour refused to put more money into them, the state of the public services deteriorated, and the time it would take to put them right grew longer. If we compare it with the only other Labour government to have had a big majority, this is what we find. In three years – just over half the time that the Blair government spent building what it considered was enough credibility to start spending money – the Attlee government of 1945–51 created the National Health Service, implemented the 1944 Education Act including raising the school leaving age and building hundreds of new schools, and created Britain's first comprehensive welfare system. All of these things it achieved between 1945 and 1948. And Attlee inherited a war-ravaged economy.

Brown would reply that, though the Attlee government's great social reforms endured, its economic record was not a success. The 1947–8 winter was a disaster: the coldest winter on record, and there was not enough food or fuel to go round. Brown the historian remembers how John Strachey was Food Minister and Emanuel Shinwell was in charge of fuel, and the justified jibe – he can quote it accurately – was 'Shiver with Shinwell and starve with Strachey'. Brown also likes to point out that he was warned against doubling the NHS budget, but did it anyway, and that he has survived a series of crises that might have derailed earlier Labour Chancellors, like the oil price crisis. If he had taken his friend Bill Keegan's advice, he thinks he and the government might not have survived.

He would also say, rightly, that the scheme for which he levied the Windfall Tax was a good and effective one: £3.5 billion, raised from the Windfall Tax, went into Welfare to Work. It paid for projects which would guarantee work or training for those aged between 18 and 25 who had been unemployed for at least six months. If they refused to take it, they could lose their welfare benefits. Employers could get £60 a week for up to 26 weeks towards recruiting and employing a jobless person. He recruited Britain's biggest businesses in aid of Welfare to Work. A business breakfast summit at 11 Downing Street brought together people like David Sainsbury, chairman of J. Sainsbury, Ian McAllister, chairman of Ford UK, and Peter Birch, chief executive of Abbey National. Brown told them they could choose whom they wished to recruit, and what wages and conditions would be – and that they could make or break Welfare to Work. All handed over written pledges to support it. The scheme could be sold to right-wing newspapers as an attack on their favourite targets, 'welfare scroungers' and 'the workshy'. For another audience, it could also be sold – as Brown sold it on the BBC's *World at One* – with an argument closer to the Chancellor's heart: 'In some communities, up to 25 per cent of the young people do not have jobs, and unemployment is so endemic that we are dealing with the third generation of families.' He would also point out that he had mounted, if not a full onslaught, at least a preliminary raid, on poverty. The main weapon in the battle to abolish child poverty was to be Brown's famous tax credits. These were payments from the government to help with everyday costs, made to people with children who work but earn low wages. Brown is the acknowledged master of the fine detail of tax credits, which played a key part in his 1998 and 1999 Budgets.

And he would also point to the national minimum wage, designed to help the lowest paid. Labour was committed to this, and Brown set up a commission under Professor George Bain, the former director of the London Business School who also had close links with the trade unions, to recommend the level. But the ever-cautious Chancellor brought in the minimum wage at a slightly lower level than Professor Bain recommended. Even so, there were those in industry who opposed it because it distorted the market. The young Gordon Brown might have pointed out that if the market required that we employ people for less money than it costs to keep body and soul together in reasonable dignity, there was something wrong with the market, but the prudent middle-aged Chancellor simply argued that, since both Labour and the Conservatives in their different ways propped up low wages with public handouts, he was saving public money by having a national minimum wage.

It is not hard to see why, so far as the trade unions were concerned, Brown was the government's friend to the working man. Blair is not a trade union type. The old vision of the labour movement – the Labour Party and the trade unions yoked together – was not one which he understood. But Brown the labour movement historian – now, that was another matter. They were not at all surprised when Brown made it clear to TUC General Secretary John Monks that he wanted to meet the unions regularly.

However, these meetings must have rung alarm bells somewhere in government circles, for according to one of the TUC's representatives at these meetings, John Edmonds, 'the day before every meeting we read the result of a briefing which said, whatever the TUC wants, they are not going to get it. After a time John Monks spoke to Gordon Brown about it and it stopped'.

The briefer, presumably, was Charlie Whelan, who had learned his trade in a decade working for the unions. After Whelan left the Treasury, a story appeared in the *Mail on Sunday* about how Whelan and Mandelson planned to expose a supposed pension fund scandal in Edmonds's union, the GMB. The next day was a scheduled meeting between Brown and the unions, and Brown said quietly to Edmonds: 'I'm sorry, I knew nothing about it.' Edmonds believes him.

Some time later Edmonds had a remarkably brief conversation with Whelan:

Whelan: 'Yeah, I did it. Well, you use what you can.' (Laughs.)
Edmonds: 'You bastard.'
Whelan: 'I'm honoured to receive that from you, John.'

Nonetheless, Brown was not doing a lot about the huge gap between richest and poorest, which has actually increased in the past ten years. The scandal, which he had attacked with vigour while in opposition, of obscene financial packages in the City, continued unchecked. Nor was he doing a lot for the unemployed, except, commendably, reducing their numbers. He told the CBI soon after the 1997 election: 'The government will restore the work ethic at the centre of our welfare state and modern employment policies … The government must ensure that hard work is encouraged and rewarded at all levels.'

In all this he was still the deeply cautious Chancellor, ensuring that he did nothing to jeopardise another election victory. But the key difference, says Edmonds, was that while both Blair and Brown took the same lessons from Labour's 1992 defeat, Blair was happy with them and Brown was not. Edmonds recalls Blair saying in his presence: 'Most of the people I went to school with are now millionaires.' William Keegan thinks Blair and Brown learned the lesson of 1992 too well, and handed the Conservatives the argument on a plate. 'The oddest thing,' writes Keegan, 'was the way the Conservatives had managed to keep the tax issue going for so long. For the whole of the 1997–2001 term Gordon

Brown was terrified of mentioning the word "tax" except to say he was against "the policies of tax and spend".' Keegan puts it down to Brown's acceptance that 'the Conservatives had won the tax argument'.[3]

In the March 2000 budget he even took a penny off the basic rate of income tax. He thought it was necessary to compensate the middle classes, because he was removing their mortgage tax relief and the allowance for married couples. But for many MPs on the benches behind him, it was the final act of betrayal. The journalist Paul Foot, admittedly a member of the Socialist Workers Party, nonetheless spoke for many Labour people when he wrote: 'Brown and Blair worked together to bring about the emasculation of the Labour government as a force for change.'[4]

Treasury officials, surprised at the apparent modesty of Brown's ambitions, seem to have been more thrown by the change in working methods. Traditional methods required officials to prepare papers and large meetings to discuss them. Brown's method was what he, Ed Balls and, most of all, Tony Blair had learned in opposition: small, fluid, informal meetings, everyone on the move, latte in one hand and mobile phone in the other, no minutes.

His cabinet colleagues found him infuriatingly interventionist. He knew that the Chancellor's control of the purse strings made him potentially the most powerful minister in the cabinet. And unlike former Chancellors, he was very hard for the Prime Minister to shift. The 1994 deal with Tony Blair gave him some rights over domestic policy, and the fact that there was a substantial minority on the Labour benches which would have preferred him to Tony Blair gave him more security of tenure. Moving Brown if Brown did not wish to be moved would have been to take a great political risk.

Education Secretaries under Blair have been in a particularly unenviable position. They had a Chancellor who wanted to know, not just that they needed money, but how they were going to spend it. But since Blair wanted to control schools policy personally, they also had a Prime Minister who wanted to control the fine detail of education policy, and had appointed his own education adviser, Andrew Adonis, whose opinion mattered more than that of any of his education secretaries. The education secretary in Blair's first term, David Blunkett, was once overheard complaining bitterly to one of his advisers: 'Someone's got to decide who's running this thing.' After a while he seems to have accepted that someone had decided, and the decision had not gone his way.

In particular, Brown wanted to see evidence that the Private Finance Initiative route was being tried for all capital expenditure. His devotion to this method of involving the private sector in public projects has been remarkable. Governments have always paid private contractors to build roads, government offices, schools, air bases, prisons and hospitals. PFI was introduced by Norman Lamont in 1992 as a way of getting capital expenditure 'off the books'. Lamont saw that if the initial capital came from a company, then future governments were actually paying, and his government was not paying – though of course in the long run the cost would be greater. Under PFI, contractors pay the construction costs and then rent the finished project back to the public sector, often for terms of 20, 25 or 30 years.

Lamont's successor Kenneth Clarke took the argument further. He said that PFI was not a matter of getting expenditure off the books, but of bringing private-sector expertise and disciplines into public-sector projects. That was how Gordon Brown saw it, too, and adherence to it was yet another way of distancing himself from traditional Labour thinking and reassuring the city. So Labour expanded PFI, despite having criticised it roundly in opposition. By the end of 2002 a total of 524 UK deals with a capital value of £23 billion were signed, for prisons, hospitals, schools, major road schemes and others, with 45 more planned. PFI by then represented 10.3 per cent of publicly-sponsored investment, according to the Institute of Fiscal Studies.

It is not just old Labour types who have doubts about this. Strategy and financial consultant Michael Mainelli has studied PFI, and wrote in 2003 that it was providing 'jam today for the government, but committing the UK public sector to significant future payments for capital projects undertaken today. At somewhere between £10 billion and £30 billion of running costs on current projections, this is a straightjacket on change in a public sector with a "managed" expenditure of £188 billion. Capital markets are beginning to note the scale and implications of PFI/PPP, but the real effect may be to affect UK attitudes to finance and government for generations. On coming to power, a new government is faced with continuing for decades the operational contracts of the previous administration's PFI/PPP, or defaulting on those contracts. The government either fails to implement its pledges or radically adjusts the risk for private sector contractors dealing with government by breaking PFI/PPP contracts. If the latter, the UK incurs increased costs for several decades in direct contracts and in debt service.'[5]

Brown left the details of PFI to Geoffrey Robinson and Ed Balls, who both thought that the rise in costs on the London Underground's Jubilee Line extension showed that the public sector could not run such projects. This was an odd conclusion to come to, because it is at least as easy to argue precisely the opposite from what happened with the Jubilee Line. First there was an unavoidable delay because of safety fears about tunnelling techniques. Then ministers suddenly demanded to have the thing ready to take passengers to the Millennium Dome on 31 December 1999. Contractors, knowing that this was the political priority, were in a strong bargaining position when it came to negotiating costs. It was the private sector, not the public sector, which pushed up costs, and they did so because they were able to do so.

Brown's devotion to PFI led to the decision which Londoners still hold against him, his refusal to allow London Mayor Ken Livingstone to handle regeneration of the London Underground. Instead he negotiated his own £13 billion PFI deal with uncharacteristic ineptness, and drove it through, against expert advice, against the will of most MPs, and overwhelmingly against the wishes of Londoners, many of whom, to this day, consider their continued suffering as the Underground regularly breaks down to be Gordon Brown's personal responsibility. When Livingstone's transport chief Bob Kiley walked out of negotiations in a bid to get the private firms he was dealing with to behave more reasonably, Brown's department ordered London Underground back to the table, and Livingstone did not have the power to countermand the order. So LU had nothing to negotiate with, since the companies knew LU was forced to do a deal with them on any terms.

Professor Tony Travers, director of the Greater London Research Unit at the LSE, commented at the time: 'The preferred bidders can add any number of noughts to the deal and wait until they get it. The government demands a quick deal at any price – any price is what they will get.' The taxpayer is putting in £1 billion a year for what increasingly looks like a shoddy repair service.

Polly Toynbee, normally a Brown supporter, wrote:

'Obliged to complete a deal, the most basic rules of commerce and competition have been abandoned … The government forgets these companies are not their friends, but obeying their duty to shareholders – not wicked, just business … Gordon Brown is an enigma to his colleagues. Very few MPs support the big PFI deals – London MPs vigorously oppose the tube PPP. Quite a few ministers mutter their disquiet. Yet they praise the remarkable good he has done on child poverty or childcare – equally all his own work.' She warned Brown that this was going to follow him around. 'Every packed platform perilously close to tipping people on to the electric lines will be down to him – when he could and should have devolved it all to the mayor. This is Gordon Brown's Groundnut Scheme, his poll tax. As with Mrs Thatcher, each impossible obstacle simply alters the stated rationale for the plan.'[6]

In this atmosphere of almost obsessive caution, there was never any chance that Brown's pledge to renationalise the railways would be kept, and it has not been. Like many omissions in the first Blair term, this has returned to cause trouble in the second and third terms.

11

The Tony and Gordon Show

When Brown takes over from Blair, there will be only one centre of power in Whitehall. Throughout the past decade, there have been two. There is no use anyone pretending that this has not hampered good government. It has.

Stories about the continued stormy relationship between the two men in government began very early, in January 1998 with the publication of Paul Routledge's biography of Brown, and have erupted from time to time ever since. Blair, say the Brownites, has betrayed deal after deal with Brown. Brown, say the Blairites, has 'psychological flaws' and should 'grow up'.[1]

In May 2000 Gordon Brown drew attention to the case of sixth former Laura Spence, from Monkseaton Community High School in Whitley Bay, Tyne and Wear, whose A-level predictions were top class, but who had been turned down at Magdelen College Oxford 'by an interview system more reminiscent of an old boy network and the old school tie than genuine justice for society'. He told a trade union gathering: 'It is about time we had an end to the old Britain, where all that matters is the privileges you were born with, rather than the potential you actually have. It is time that these old universities opened their doors to women and people from all backgrounds.' At the time, a quarter of all university students came from the 7 per cent of the population which attended private schools; this rose to a third in the prestigious Russell Group universities, and about a half in Oxford and Cambridge. (Today, seven years on, the figures do not look much different.)

Blair supported Brown publicly, but inspired leaks revealed that he was embarrassed and angry. He thought that it sounded dreadfully Old Labour. He also wondered suspiciously whether it was a sly way of drawing attention to the fact that Blair went from public school to Oxford with comparatively indifferent A-levels, and may have benefited from precisely the snobbery his Chancellor was attacking.

Blair was also shaken by the outrage Brown's speech evoked from the President of Magdelen, Professor Anthony Smith, who claimed that comprehensive school teachers were telling their pupils not to apply. There is an unexpected connection between Smith and Brown. In the 1980s, Professor Smith was director of the British Film Institute. When he left to go to Magdelen, he was succeeded by his deputy, Brown's old friend Wilf Stevenson, now director of the Smith Institute and likely to play a key role in 10 Downing Street when Brown gets there.

Labour's second term began in June 2001 with another Labour landslide against a new Conservative leader, William Hague, who had consistently excelled in the House of Commons but conspicuously failed to unite his warring party. Labour had a slightly reduced majority of 166 (down from 179). The Conservatives took one extra seat, and the Liberal Democrats six to win 52 seats, their highest since 1929. Blair considered forcing his Chancellor to move to the Foreign Office, which he knew Brown would resist, and decided against it. He did, however, take the Foreign Office away from Robin Cook, whom the new Bush administration in Washington did not entirely like, replacing him with Jack Straw.

At last, Brown started to think it might be possible to persuade the Prime Minister that the very richest might pay direct tax of more than 40 pence in the pound. He was wrong. In June 2003, the new Leader of the House of Commons, Peter Hain, intended in a speech to say that the top rate of 40 per cent 'now catches too many middle income employees, including teachers and police', and to wonder aloud whether therefore a new top rate might be appropriate for the richest. It reflected Brown's thinking, and he was dismayed when Blair firmly vetoed Hain's speech.

Labour's manifesto promised 'investment and reform' in public services, as well as to 'engage fully in Europe' and 'help enlarge the European Union' but the British people would have 'the final say in any proposal to join the euro' by way of a referendum. This masked a new conflict between Blair and Brown. By now, Blair wanted to join the single currency. But back in 1997, Brown had laid down his 'five economic tests' which had to be passed before there would be any proposal upon which the people might vote.

There must be 'sustainable convergence' between Britain and the other economies (Britain's business cycle was out of line with that of other EU countries). There must be flexibility to cope with economic change, and it must be good for investment, Britain's financial services industry, and employment.

This looked like being the issue of the moment until, on 11 September 2001, two passenger aeroplanes were deliberately flown into the world's highest buildings, the two towers of the World Trade Centre in New York. Another went into the Pentagon in Washington, and a fourth crashed after passengers attacked the hijackers. The terms of their 1994 deal required Blair to give Brown a pretty free rein on domestic issues – but required Brown to leave Blair alone on the world stage. The strategy that emerged in the first few days after the attack on the World Trade Centre was Blair's. We do not know for certain what Brown thought of it, and we will not know until they are both out of office; but as we shall see, there are some fairly clear indications.

Less than a month after 9/11, Britain and the USA were bombing Afghanistan. Kabul fell on 13 November, and in January 2002 the first of hundreds of chained and hooded people were herded onto a US cargo jet and flown to Guantanamo Bay on the island of Cuba. As I write, six years later, we are little nearer knowing what crimes they are suspected of, what evidence there is that they ever committed them, what methods have been used to humiliate them and extract confessions from them, or when, if ever, they will be released. We do know that some of them are British citizens, and that their Prime Minister does not seem very concerned about whether they will receive justice. A search for the weapons of mass destruction which were the justification for the invasion of Iraq produced nothing, but Blair agreed at a meeting with President Bush that Britain would accompany the USA into the war.

It took Brown a long time to announce that he supported the war – so long that it became the subject of comment. It was a dilemma for him, says one of his closest political allies. 'Tony Blair made the decisions and brought ministers together on them. Gordon was never a spokesperson on the war. Blair did not want him to be one. Pressed, he would say things, but never enough to outweigh those who said he was not saying enough.' The famous 'Macavity' charge – that Brown was like T S Eliot's cat, never there when the crime is discovered – is bitterly resented by the Brownites: 'He wasn't there because Blair didn't want him there, until it started to get tough and he needed him there.'

Iraq, as even the most loyal Blairites are starting to acknowledge, has been the big disaster of the Blair premiership, and the question of whether Brown would have averted it, and whether his relationship with the Americans will be a more equal one than Blair's, is key to understanding the future under Prime Minister Brown. Neil Kinnock told me: 'It's conceivable that Gordon would have wanted the detail of post-war planning in indelible ink as the *quid pro quo* for committing British forces.' You can read that sentence without the first three words. Kinnock talks to Brown regularly.

'This is because he's built in a way that says, what matters is what happens afterwards.' says Kinnock. 'That's Gordon, that's the negotiator, that's can we afford the mortgage, and it's a very necessary political trait.' This is a fascinating comment, because it's nearer than Kinnock normally gets to criticising Tony Blair. It seems very likely that the infinitely cautious Brown would at least have insisted on seeing and agreeing the plan for post war reconstruction before committing British troops.

Another senior politician close to Brown is sure he would also have wanted a final report from Hans Blix's UN weapons inspectors before committing troops. Brown's friend and adviser Wilf Stevenson thinks a Brown government would have insisted on Iraq having time to comply with the UN resolution – which might well have meant not going in, because before the war Saddam Hussein was clearly on the run, permitting, for example, the humiliation of UN inspectors searching his palaces without notice.

Brown, says Kinnock, would have been able to resist Bush's blandishments with confidence, because of 'his long and deep familiarity with the USA and its political class, including Alan Greenspan. No one could accuse him of being anti-American.' Gordon Brown's disciple Nick Brown now wishes he had resigned from the cabinet with Robin Cook rather than vote for the war. The two Browns kept in touch all the way through, and reached the decision early that there was going to be a war.

Once Blair was committed, says Kinnock, 'it was hard to get any proportionate reciprocal response from the White House. It was too great fidelity. All that served a practical end until we got to the end of the Iraq war, when it became evident that the Americans had not only made no preparations but had actually torn up the plans prepared by Colin Powell. That pulled a large rug from under Tony's feet. His dilemma then was: sustain the engagement to try against the odds to influence, or try to step back from it. He thought stepping back would endanger his credibility. I don't think it would, but I'm certain that was his reasoning.'

'The relationship with George Bush would have been different with Gordon as PM', says one of Brown's key advisers. 'There would have been an independent British foreign policy – and perhaps an independent British Foreign Secretary too, which we have never had under Blair.'

The Iraq war marked the moment when the veteran socialist Michael Foot started to lose patience with New Labour, according to his biographer Kenneth Morgan: 'It was in its almost total lack of interest in history that "New Labour" in his own later years seemed to him most culpably deficient and spiritually dead, Gordon Brown being a distinguished exception. He was not reassured by the spectacle of Tony Blair proclaiming that "I feel the hand of history on our shoulders" or telling the American Congress that "history will forgive" the invasion of Iraq. Dragging in the endorsement of Almighty God was even worse.'[2]

On 18 March 2003, in a televised address, Bush gave Saddam Hussein 48 hours to leave Iraq or face invasion. The war began two days later, and on 9 April, US troops helped crowds to topple a giant statue of Saddam Hussein in the heart of Baghdad. Widespread looting broke out unhindered in the Iraqi capital. Four years later, what is happening in Baghdad is a lot worse than looting.

Apart from the fact that, in their great 1994 carve-up, foreign affairs had fallen to Blair, there was another reason why Gordon Brown was not prominent in the build-up to war. In July 2002 he and Sarah had announced the imminent arrival of their first child. His wife announced that she was giving up her directorship of Hobsbawm Macaulay and would take at least several months off work. They had been married quietly the previous year in Fife by the Reverend Sheila Munro, minister for the parishes of Inverkeithing and North Queensferry, and had managed to keep it secret until the day itself, when newspapers were allowed to photograph them after the ceremony.

On 28 December 2002 Jennifer Jane Brown was born at Forth Park hospital, Fife, seven weeks prematurely, two months before her father's 51st birthday, weighing 2lbs 4oz. Despite being so early and so small, it looked at first as though she would be healthy, and six days later Sarah Brown left the hospital with her husband, saying that they expected their daughter to be able to come home in five or six weeks. But Jennifer died after a brain haemorrhage when she was 10 days old, in the arms of her parents, at Edinburgh Royal Infirmary. The day before her death, already knowing the worst, the Browns arranged for her to be baptised by a Church of Scotland minister in a short, private ceremony at her incubator.

Political colleagues paid tribute, mostly sounding stiff and formal – it is very hard to devise a statement that does justice to the death of a child. Ironically it was only the old foe Tony Blair, with that precious gift he has of striking the right note, who managed a statement that meant something. In Afghanistan, audibly emotional, he said: 'I feel so desperately sorry for Gordon and Sarah. I know how much Gordon was looking forward to being a father. I know how proud they both were of Jennifer Jane and I know what wonderful parents they would have been to her ...'

Jennifer, said Brown, changed his life: 'I don't think we will be the same again.' His religion became a more important part of his life. He sat down to write a book, *Courage*, described in Chapter 16, which will be published this summer just as he becomes Prime Minister (the timing, he insists, is accidental). It is dedicated to Jennifer, and his royalties will go to the charity he and Sarah set up in her name for research at Edinburgh into the illness from which she died. He could not listen to music for nearly a year after Jennifer Jane died. And even today, when he mentions her in any context – for example to tell you that this was what made him sit down and write *Courage* – it is an effort of will to say her name, and you can sense the tears beneath the surface. His son John was born in October 2003, weighing a healthy 8lb 1oz, and named after Brown's late father Dr John Brown. After the birth the Chancellor pronounced himself part of the 'happiest family in Britain'. He added: 'There are sleepless nights but there is a spring in my step every morning.'

Late in 2003, Brown and Blair patched up an agreement, papering

over the differences between them. Brown wanted to rule the euro out
for that parliament; Blair wanted to leave the door open. They left it
half open. Blair could return to the subject, but with no hope at all
that Brown might take a different view. Before that, Blair had tried a
desperate stratagem. He asked Clare Short to tell Brown that, if only
Brown would let him join the euro, he would resign in Brown's favour.
She conveyed the message. Brown said he had already heard the same
from two other messengers; that this was no way to make policy; and
that anyway, he no longer believed Blair would keep his word.[3] Blair also
asked his aide Anji Hunter to make the offer, and then made it himself
over dinner alone with Brown. It was again turned down. 'History would
never forgive us for having that conversation', said Brown.[4]

2003 was Brown's seventh year at the Treasury, and the year he
became the longest serving Chancellor of the Exchequer since Nicholas
Vansittart (1812–23). He did not covet Vansittart's 11-year record. It
was time, he thought, to move onto better things. Blair did not agree.
The next year, 2004, Blair's former economic adviser Derek Scott published his memoirs, which contained a sustained attack on the Chancellor. Just as the Blairites insisted that Paul Routledge's book had been
authorised by Brown in order to cause trouble, so now the Brownites
made the same allegation about Scott's book. Did Blair support Scott's
allegations – in particular the damaging one that Brown was warned
his withdrawal of tax credits on pension funds would cause a pensions
crisis? The parliamentary press lobby tried to get a straight answer from
the Prime Minister's official spokeswoman (PMS) and she wriggled like a
true professional. The official report of her lobby briefing begins:

> 'Asked by the *Evening Standard* if there was an "orchestrated cam-
> paign" by Downing Street to discredit the Chancellor and the Treas-
> ury, the PMS said that she presumed she was being questioned
> about Derek Scott's book. Put to her that she was being asked if
> Downing Street agreed with the Chancellor' s statement, the PMS

said that the Chancellor's spokesman's statement had been referring to the contents of Mr Scott's book. She underlined that the
book had been totally unauthorised and pointed out that such
books were only written to make money and cause trouble and division. As far as we were concerned, however, Mr Scott's book would
not cause any division. She would also caution journalists against
believing everything they read. Asked if she was confirming that the
book contained descriptions of clashes between the Prime Minister
and the Chancellor, the PMS said no. She was simply responding to
questions being asked about the issue …'

Two more big issues in the 2001–2005 parliament divided Prime
Minister and Chancellor: foundation hospitals, and plans to charge
tuition fees to students. In both cases, Brown seemed to be aligned
with Labour traditionalists unhappy with a Blair policy – though, as
often happens with this complex, cautious and subtle man, things were
not quite as simple as that.

Foundation hospitals were to be hospitals that opted out of government control and became independent not-for-profit organisations,
able to borrow money on the private markets and set their own financial and clinical priorities. Early in 2003, about 100 Labour MPs signed
a Commons motion opposing the policy, including several former ministers and MPs usually loyal to the prime minister. They said foundation
hospitals would create a two-tier NHS, where some patients would get
the best treatment from the best funded hospitals able to offer higher
salaries to get the best staff, and other patients would get second rate
treatment. Coming on top of the bitter rebellion over the Iraq war, this
had the potential to damage Blair seriously. Blair and his Health Secretary Alan Milburn needed Brown. And they were not sure they had him.
Brown worried about foundation hospitals borrowing on the private
markets for major projects, running up large debts, and relying on the
Treasury to bail them out. In the end, the controversial health and

social care bill, which contained plans to introduce foundation hospitals, passed its second reading on 7 May 2003, but only with a greatly reduced government majority of 74 and a substantial Labour rebellion. One of the rebels, former Labour Health Secretary Frank Dobson, told the Commons that foundation hospitals would 'set hospital against hospital'.

The next year, 2004, came top-up fees. The Labour Party had reluctantly swallowed the idea of charging tuition fees to students. Most Labour MPs had benefited from free higher education in their youth, and in the early 1970s the student Rector of Edinburgh University, Gordon Brown, had campaigned for higher grants to go with them. Labour MPs had swallowed the pill – but on the basis that the fee was capped at a low level, and standard throughout higher education. Now they were being asked to accept variable fees, and a much higher cap, so that it might, say, become very expensive to go to Blair's old college, St John's College, Oxford; less so to go to Edinburgh University, his Chancellor's alma mater; and for those who couldn't afford an ancient university at all, it would be dead cheap to go to a former polytechnic.

The left-wing MP Ian Gibson was a predictable rebel leader, saying 'The cap will rise and the division between rich and poor institutions will widen.' Less predictably, a key figure was Brown's long-standing friend and ally, Nick Brown. This, said the Blairites, was rank proof of the Chancellor's perfidy. Was it not well known that when Gordon said 'jump' Nick asked 'how high?' As Kevin Maguire put it in *The Guardian*: 'If Nick Brown is a rebel with a cause, the cause is the crowning of Gordon Brown as prime minister rather than halting university top-up fees.'[5] Since 1997, Blairite bullets aimed at Gordon had found their way to Nick. He was blamed for telling Brown biographer Paul Routledge that Tony Blair had stolen the leadership. He was moved to Agriculture, where he was nominally in charge during the foot and mouth crisis, and took the blame when it went wrong, though in fact Blair took most of the decisions out of his hands. He was outed as gay by a former boyfriend in the *News of the World* – it was known in Westminster, but Nick Brown had hoped to avoid publicity because he had not told his elderly mother. He believes Blair's spin doctor Alastair Campbell had something to do with the *News of the World*'s decision to publish. When Peter Mandelson was forced to resign after the revelation of the home loan he had received from Geoffrey Robinson, Nick Brown was accused by Blairites of revealing the story. He was demoted after the 2001 election, but the Chancellor managed to save his friend's cabinet seat until 2003 when he was consigned to the back benches, from where he led the revolt over top-up fees. He was vital to it. There are not enough left-wingers like Dr Gibson to rebel with a chance of success. It needed Nick Brown (who had never rebelled before) and those MPs willing to take their lead from him. And in the end, a relatively minor concession was enough to get him to vote with the government. His decision saved the government, which scraped home by just five votes, 316 votes to 311. Where was Gordon Brown in all this? Angry Blairites, including Charles Clarke, believed that he was pulling Nick Brown's strings. But Nick Brown insists he chose the path of rebellion against Gordon's wishes, and Gordon's contribution was to help get Nick into the government lobby in the end.

The key vote, in January 2004, came shortly before the publication of Lord Hutton's report on the Iraq affair and the suicide of weapons inspector David Kelly, so a defeat would have been very serious. 'Gordon strongly wanted to keep the government together', Nick Brown told me. 'He always opposed the rebellion. It suited the Blairites to say he encouraged me, but he did not. He personally saved the government by phoning all of us. I was expressing my point of view; Gordon had a different point of view.' The general view of Nick Brown's eventual decision to vote with the government was well expressed by Kevin Maguire: 'His startling conversion on the road to the lobby owed more to intense pressure applied by the politician he champions than any concessions offered by the government. The former Chief Whip must calculate, speculated a close friend and admirer yesterday, that his personal embarrassment is a price worth paying if it helps the Chancellor to the Labour leadership.'[6] Not so, says Nick Brown: 'I thought the concessions I had were worth having. If the government had lost, it intended to put the whole scheme through on a confidence vote, shorn of all the concessions. The alternative to voting for that would have been to bring down the government.'

Whether you see Gordon Brown as the man who caused the trouble for the government in the first place, or the man who saved the government, depends, like so much else, on whether you believe in the Brown or Blair version of history.

12

The End of the Tony and Gordon Show

Tony Blair and Gordon Brown take a stroll through the park together. 'Look', says Tony, 'Let's be honest with one another'. 'Sure', says Gordon, 'You go first'. And that was the end of the conversation.

It's a joke, of course, recycled by Anthony Giddens in his book *Over To You Gordon*, but there's a grim reality behind it. Brown believes that Blair, by leading Labour into the 2005 election, betrayed a clear unwritten understanding. In 1994, Blair, he believes, promised to resign during his second term and support Brown as his successor. He repeated this promise more than once during the 2002–2005 parliament, and repeatedly reneged on it.

Whatever the truth of that, there certainly was a deal that Brown would have overlordship of the domestic agenda. This one was in writing, and Blair certainly did break it before the 2005 general election, taking back as much as he could, and then trying to shift Brown from the Treasury. He offered Brown pretty well anything else he fancied. He could have the Foreign Office. He could be Deputy Prime Minister and chair of all committees dealing with domestic policy. Brown, I'm told, accepted this second idea, saying he was willing to do all that and stay as Chancellor too. This, it turned out, was not what Tony Blair had in mind. I have a dark suspicion that Brown knew that.

Relations grew poisonous. In 2004 there were several attempts at peacemaking by the Deputy Prime Minister John Prescott. One, bizarrely in the back seat of Prescott's official black Jaguar, in the car park of the Loch Fyne Oyster Bar in Argyll after a memorial service marking the tenth anniversary of John Smith's death, hit the headlines when it was leaked. To complete the surreal scene, another official car was parked, behind them, containing Health Secretary John Reid and his junior minister Douglas Alexander. But it cannot have been a very significant talk. Brown's memory of the occasion is that he spent most of the time on the telephone to his dying mother in Aberdeenshire, with whom he spent most of that summer, forgoing his usual trip to Cape Cod. She was dead before the year ended.

In July 2004, Blair told Brown he was minded to stand down in a few weeks time. No one, on either side, disputes this. Brown did not believe it, and he was right. The most loyal cabinet Blairites – Tessa Jowell, Charles Clarke, John Reid, Patricia Hewitt – stiffened Blair's spine, but not quite enough. In September, Blair made a clear, unambiguous public statement from which it has proved impossible to retreat. No Prime Minister in history has ever done anything like it. He announced that he would lead his party into the next general election; that he would serve 'a full third term'; but he would not lead his party into the subsequent election. It was not done from strength. It was done at a time when, however determined Blair was to stay, there was a question mark over his survival. The Butler Report on the Iraq War, due out at that time, might have sunk him.

Blair's announcement, as Robert Peston puts it, was 'the long-anticipated serving of the divorce papers on Brown. Their dysfunctional marriage is now at an end … Brown remains as Chancellor for no other reason than that it is too dangerous for Blair to sack him. The formal dismissal of Brown would trigger a revolt among Labour MPs that would probably do for Blair … The occasional meetings they have now are stilted, characterised by the withholding of information rather than the sharing of confidences.' Peston revealed that Brown routinely says to Blair: 'There is nothing you could ever say to me now that I could ever believe.' Blair's friends say Brown has been obstructive and difficult, over tuition fees and over entry to the euro, and could be Prime Minister today if he had given Blair the unconditional loyalty Blair wanted.

Peston also quotes Brown as calling this 'a liberating moment'.[1] I think that with each passing month since then, it has become clearer what Brown meant by 'liberating'. Right up to that moment, there had been a shared project. He and Blair have very different instincts, but both believed in the same prescription in 1997. That has become progressively less true.

Brown was willing to be Blair's natural successor, if Blair was going to organise things in the way that he thought they had agreed. But now the deal was off. Brown's mistake – a surprising one for a historian – was to forget that politicians simply do not give up the premiership once they have it. There was not going to be any orderly, friendly passing of power from Blair to Brown.

Blair's intention of serving a full third term and then resigning at the end of it would give Brown and the Labour Party the worst of all possible worlds. The new leader would have no time establish himself. He could only present himself at the following general election as Tony Blair Mark Two, and would probably go down to a heavy defeat. Blair and Blairism would be the sole beneficiary of all the work Labour people had done to make their Party electable again. Why should Brown or the Labour Party stand for it? Blair had to be forced out earlier than he planned.

The method of the announcement did not help, either, giving the impression of deliberately rubbing salt in the wound. As often happens with Blair, the story was leaked exclusively to *The Sun* well before the announcement was made. Brown saw it in that paper, asked Blair, and was told it was untrue. A few days later, the Butler enquiry cleared Blair of deliberate distortion over the Iraq war. If it had not done so, it would have been hard to announce that he was going to lead Labour into the election. As it was, he made the announcement the tabloid had predicted.

It became even clearer to Brown that all hope of a peaceful transition was gone when Blair brought Alan Milburn back into the cabinet, and gave him Brown's usual job of heading the general election campaign. Brown and Milburn had quarrelled bitterly over health policy when Milburn was Health Secretary, and Milburn is one of the pathological Brown-haters round Blair, alongside Clarke, Hewitt, Reid and Jowell.

The moment was coming when Brown would have to unleash those forces he had shrunk from releasing in 1994. It was not just a question of Brown wanting Blair's job – though he does, so badly he can almost taste it. It was also that Brown still believes Labour is the Party of the underdog. There was much policy agreement between them. But there was always that fundamental difference. Brown – as Neil Kinnock likes saying – has 'Labour' written all the way through him. Blair is still, even after all these years, seen as a cuckoo in Labour's nest.

Brown's new strategy emerged at the 2004 Labour conference, after *The Sun* had leaked Blair's intentions but before Blair's announcement. It was to position himself as the man who espoused at least some of Labour's traditional ideas and values, as against divisive and cynical politicians like Blair and Milburn, and to start expressing his growing but still heretical conviction that the market has limitations. 'There are values far beyond those of contracts, markets and exchange', he told the delegates. 'Public service can be a calling and not just a career.' It was a tremendous speech, and it was also a public statement of what everyone knew, that the marriage was over.

Brown is said to believe that Blair wants to preserve his legacy by making sure Brown cannot be a successful Prime Minister; that Blair and Mandelson are doing on a grand scale what Mandelson did on a much smaller one when he left the job of Director of Communications at Labour Party headquarters before the 1987 election, and used his access to Neil Kinnock and the press lobby to undermine his successor and effectively destroy the Party's campaigning ability.

Brown's friend Wilf Stevenson goes even further. He believes that Iraq has lengthened Blair's tenure, because he has hung on – and Brown has let him hang on – in the hope that Iraq will come right, to improve his legacy. Whether that is so or not, it seems to me likely that Blair could not have survived without Brown. Blair's feel for the party he led was always an uncertain one. Left to himself, he would probably have overreached. But he was not left to himself, at least on the domestic front. His ideas had to jump the hurdle of the Chancellor. Just as when Blair was Shadow Home Secretary, Brown stopped him from going out with the unadorned slogan 'tough on crime' and persuaded him to add 'and tough on the causes of crime', so Brown played that role for Blair throughout his premiership. He saved Blair from himself.

As the election drew closer, relations worsened almost daily. Brown did not rage about the appointment of Alan Milburn ahead of him to run the election campaign; he just ignored Milburn, making his own arrangements for a campaign tour with no reference to him. Blair's and Brown's public appearances were no longer co-ordinated, because they were not on speaking terms, and Brown thought Blair was timing his press conferences with a view to upstaging the Chancellor. The Conservatives toyed with the idea of putting on their posters the Brown line revealed by Peston – 'There is nothing you could ever say to me now that I could ever believe' – and also producing posters that said 'Vote Blair, get Brown', but their focus groups told them they would backfire. Blair's stock was so low, and Brown's so high, that getting Brown would be an incentive to vote Labour.

But in the end, Blair and Brown are professional politicians. When the election campaign came, they sat on platforms together, and smiled at each other. Blair called Brown 'the most successful Chancellor for 100 years' and you would never have known that a matter of weeks earlier he had been telling his closest friends that after the election he intended to move Brown out of the Treasury. Brown said of Blair's decision to go to war in Iraq: 'I not only trust Tony Blair but I respect Tony

Blair for the way he went about that decision' and no one would have known that he was not at all happy with the decision, and did not trust his leader an inch.

Labour won a third full term in government, with a reduced majority of 66, despite the Iraq war, despite the growing aura of sleaze surrounding the Prime Minister, despite the now well known fact that Prime Minister and Chancellor were hardly on speaking terms. Nonetheless, the curtain had come down on the Gordon and Tony Show, not just because they have conflicting ambitions, but also because in the last analysis they believe different things.

13

The Search for
Notgordon Brown

By 2006 Blair was a doomed Prime Minister. If he had to go, he was determined to stamp as much of his political philosophy on Britain as he could. He returned from the election determined to create trust schools.

It was a similar idea to foundation hospitals, and attacked on much the same grounds. He was bringing into schools a far more decisive role for the private sector, for business and for churches and other 'faith groups', and allowing them to select a proportion of their pupil intake. Labour left-wingers claimed Blair had effectively resigned from the Labour Party and become the leader of a government of national coalition. He had become a Ramsay MacDonald figure; and the Labour Party knows no worse insult.

Blair has put money into education, but spent it in ways that offend the deepest instincts of Labour's traditional supporters, for example by protecting the hated 11-plus in those areas, like Kent and Buckinghamshire, where it still exists, and by bringing in, for the first time, the principle that students pay for higher education, and then a refinement – top-up fees – designed to ensure that the best universities cost more.

Even Blair's old boss Neil Kinnock publicly attacked trust schools – the only time he has ever criticized any of his successors. Only on education could Blair have brought out the old Neil Kinnock. Kinnock has known all his life that he is a product of the 1944 Education Act. He famously once asked the Labour Party conference rhetorically why he was 'the first Kinnock for 1,000 generations' to have a university education. He fought for comprehensive schools. 'Nobody who has observed a community that operates a selective eleven plus system, can doubt that on the morning of the results there are ... floods of tears in many homes.' He privately hated tuition fees, comforting himself with the thought that when Blair went, Kinnock's old friend Charles Clarke would change the system (this was before Clarke started to self-destruct). When he talked to me for this book, Kinnock also said: 'Tony never used to wear his religion on his sleeve in the way he does now. I did not know he was a believer at first. It emerged over the years as a central characteristic and his devoutness has become more apparent. It has distorted government education policy.'

Yet Gordon Brown went to a lot of trouble to persuade those MPs over whom he had some influence to vote for trust schools. You could not have a clearer indication of Brown's determination to inherit a united party. Brown must know that the decision to focus on trust schools seemed to be Blair's gesture of contempt for a party he considers not worthy of him. Brown also knew that it was his best chance ever of dislodging Blair, for it was an issue on which many mainstream Labour MPs would support Brown if he gave a lead. Opponents of trust schools included Neil Kinnock and even John Prescott, as well as the former Education Secretary Estelle Morris. They even included the old loyalist Alastair Campbell, who was pleased to be reported clapping loudly as Kinnock laid into the plan.

As Polly Toynbee wrote in *The Guardian*, 'A muddled reform, moving further in the direction that Blair has already dragged his reluctant, but until now obedient, party, was absurdly overhyped as "the most radical since the 1944 Education Act". That ignited all the suppressed disquiet about specialist schools, academies, faith schools and – now – blurred admissions procedures. He is leading the party into a cul-de-sac where it will be lose-lose for Labour and win-win for the Tories … The leader with no future and nothing to lose taunts those with their party's long-term survival at heart. But if it all ends badly, he will, for all his triumphs, rightly be reviled as the man who threw it all away.'

It was another dreadful dilemma for Brown. If he had fought Blair publicly over trust schools and threatened resignation, he would probably have won. But he judged that the price of inheriting the leadership in such conditions was too great, for it required him to place himself in a position where he would look like the triumphal return of old Labour. It was the Brown style of decision-making again, and again it prevented him from taking the throne.

Despite his efforts, for the first time the rebellion on the Labour benches was so significant that Blair relied on Conservative votes to get his legislation through. Conservative education spokesman David Willetts had a point when he said: 'Tonight has shown a divided Labour party that can't deliver public service reform, and a united Conservative party that can.'

Nonetheless, for a lame duck Prime Minister, Blair did well in the first months of the new parliament. In July 2005, the choice of London to host the 2012 Olympic Games was a personal triumph for his persuasive and diplomatic skill. The very next day, suicide bombers launched fatal attacks on the London Underground, a situation which saw Blair at his best, instinctively finding the right things to say and the right way to behave.

The better he did, the more Blair regretted having tied himself to leaving before the next general election, and thought there might be a way of escaping from the commitment. Brown was determined not to take over in the dying weeks of a parliament, with no time to establish his own style of premiership. So the debilitating battle inside government started all over again.

Brown's and Blair's speeches to the 2005 Labour conference underlined their differences, Brown sounding like a man with renewed determination to fight for the underdog and Blair proclaiming choice and markets. Blair fought to embed policies that Brown might dislike but would not be able to jettison – not just trust schools, but also greater private sector involvement in healthcare, detaining terrorist suspects without trial, and limiting the scope of incapacity benefit. Blair told friends he did not want to quit until 2008 at the earliest. For Brown, it was the best of times; it was the worst of times.

2006 began with 'one of the Prime Minister's closest allies' – an unnamed 'former cabinet minister' – saying that Brown would drag Labour back to the past, while Conservative leader David Cameron was saying, 'I think [Brown] is very much a 1980s politician'.[1] Brown could be forgiven for thinking that the Blairites were allying with the Conservatives to damage him. By the end of the month, Cameron was claiming to be the natural heir to Tony Blair. It was an acute dilemma for Brown. If he did not distance himself from Blair, then he was vulnerable to the question why, apart from personal ambition, he wished to replace him. But if he did distance himself from Blair, then the two-pronged attack from Cameron and the Blairites might sink him electorally. He feared opening up all the splits that he has been trying hard to avoid ever since 1994. He wanted Blair to go early, and endorse him.

Several meetings between the two failed to resolve the question. Meanwhile Brown, in a planned series of speeches, was carefully setting out his stall on matters outside his Treasury remit, trying, not always successfully, to sound at one and the same time different from Blair, and Blair's natural successor. So in June came his sudden declaration of support for the renewal of Britain's nuclear deterrent, in his Mansion House speech. He only used five words in passing – 'retaining our independent nuclear deterrent' – but it was enough to infuriate the Labour left. It was surprising because Brown would far rather spend taxes on tax credits or public services. Blair, on the other hand, is likely to echo the famous declaration of Labour's foreign secretary in the 1945 government, Ernest Bevin: 'We've got to have this thing. We've got to have the bloody Union Jack on it.'

Then Brown told the Royal United Services Institute : 'Address-ing the reality and causes of international terrorism is the great new challenge of our times. Upon succeeding in meeting this challenge, all else depends. So it is right to begin a series of speeches I make about how the Britain of the future will meet the global challenges ahead by addressing this question pre-eminent to our foreign defence and law and order policies, at the core of the very security and safety of our country and vital to the prosperity and future of our country. There is a common thread running through the new security challenges, and that is the growing importance, and the obvious vulnerability, of identity.' He backed identity cards, longer periods of detention without charge and faster extradition procedures, and echoed the Home Office line by saying that the 28-day limit, set by the Commons, on the time a suspect can be held before they are charged or released was insuf-ficient. He also said he wanted the 'glorification of terrorism' clause in the government's terror bill to be reinstated. This was enough to encourage Brown's old enemy, the embattled Home Secretary Charles Clarke, along with Defence Secretary John Reid, to think of Brown briefly as a man they could work with.

It was all so brief. Within days our old friends the 'Blair confidantes' started talking Brown down again, and saying they wanted a serious challenger for the leadership to emerge. 'It's been a good week for Tony, so Gordon will no doubt sulk for a bit. Then he'll come back again' one of them told *The Guardian*. Clarke and Reid were telling Blair not to hurry away. Both saw themselves as possible challengers to Brown.

The starkness of Brown's dilemma was illustrated when the trans-port workers' leader Tony Woodley – arguably the most influential union leader in the country – said: 'It's important that we see Brown's own stamp on our party and understand his own personal policies here. A "Blair Two" isn't the answer, it's a "Brown One" or "Whoever One" with policies we can all get behind.'[2] A heavyweight voice from the past also weighed in in Brown's support. Tony Blair was losing his grip and should stand down in favour of Brown at once, said former Chancellor Denis Healey, now Lord Healey, on BBC1's *Sunday* AM: 'Over the last two years, with the intervention in Iraq, then university entrance fees and foundation hospitals, I think Tony's showing he is losing his grip, and the sooner Gordon takes over the better.'

Blair's troubles, and his alienation from his Party, were deepening. Then came further damaging revelations about the extent to which wealthy people had 'loaned' the Labour Party money, and were subsequently offered peerages. The Labour Party treasurer, the transport workers' Deputy General Secretary Jack Dromey, went public with the news that he had never been consulted. On 21 March police began a 13-month investigation into secret loans to the Labour Party totalling £14 million – they submitted their report to the Crown Prosecution Service on 20 April 2007.

In the midst of it all, Blair told the world that he regretted his decision to say that he would leave before the next election, while his supporters accused Brown of deliberately sabotaging Labour's local election campaign. They said that in the March budget, Brown's withdrawal of a £200 council tax discount for pensioners was designed to damage Labour. 'The Blair-Brown marriage has reached the broken crockery stage' wrote *The Guardian*'s political editor Michael White. 'The Blairite provisional wing are destructive wreckers' was the headline over Polly Toynbee's *Guardian* comment on these events. Brown admitted publicly that he had no idea when Blair intended to leave office, and claimed unconvincingly that he never gave it a moment's thought, being far too busy with his duties as Chancellor.

Perhaps he gave it less thought than he might have done a few years earlier. Throughout 2006 at least a part of the Chancellor's mind was absorbed by yet another family misfortune. His second son, Fraser, was born in July, and soon afterwards was diagnosed with cystic fybrosis, which is caused by an abnormal gene inherited from both parents. Average life expectancy for sufferers is 31, and they suffer from recurrent chest infections. About one in 2,500 babies are born with the condition, the most common severe inherited disorder among white Europeans and north Americans. When *The Sun* got the story in November, a statement was released saying that Sarah and Gordon Brown 'are confident that the advice and treatments available, including proper exercise and, later, sporting activity will keep him fit and healthy. The NHS is doing a great job, and Gordon and Sarah are very optimistic that the advances being made in medicine will help him and many others, and they hope to be able to play their part in doing what they can to help others.'

Blair and Brown staggered through the summer, constantly sniping, retreating, withdrawing, publicly telling the world that all was peace and privately encouraging their lieutenants to say damaging things about each other. It has to be said that the Blairites were more thoroughgoing in this latter activity, with an unstoppable stream of non-attributable venom directed at the Chancellor from 'ministers close to Tony Blair' and 'long-standing friends of the Prime Minister' and 'former cabinet ministers' (the last generally thought to be Alan Milburn), appearing under the bylines of journalists whom insiders knew to have particularly good contacts in Blairite circles, like Patrick Wintour of *The Guardian* and Andrew Grice of *The Independent*.

In this fetid atmosphere, the most loyal ally could find himself denounced as a traitor for a minor deviation from the line, rather like Stalin's inner circle in the 1930s. The ultra-loyal Blairite Charles Clarke, fired (perhaps a little unfairly) as Home Secretary after his admission that 1,023 foreign prisoners were released without being considered for deportation, found himself on the receiving end of a non-attributable kicking. His crime was to say that Blair should stay at least until 2008, as he wished to do – but only if he could recover his 'sense of direction, leadership and purpose'.

Brown's closest political friend Ed Balls was sent out to tell the world that it would all come right in the end. 'It is more than 15 years since Margaret Thatcher went, but the Tory party has still not really recovered, so everyone in our party has a responsibility to get this transition right,' he told *Observer* readers on 3 September. Yes, 'these have been a tough few weeks', but the economy was still strong and he added hopefully that Labour 'is not ideologically split or fundamentally divided on principles'.

Just two days later, Blair and Brown sat in 10 Downing Street and had as furious a row as they had ever had. It lasted for three and a half hours. Brown demanded that Blair was to tell 'Blair confidantes' to stop dripping poison. He wanted an end to talk of a Blair-led 'fundamental debate about the Labour Party's future', since he had come to the pretty inevitable conclusion that this was a way of tying a Brown premiership to a Blair agenda. He demanded a timetable for Blair's departure – not a private one, but a public one, for otherwise he did not trust the Prime Minister to deliver. He wanted Blair gone by Christmas. Blair's staff, with Blair's authority, told journalists Brown was trying to blackmail him.

Similar demands were coming from unexpected sections of the party, including Blair loyalists on the back benches. Ministers started to resign, and more resignations were threatened. Fifteen MPs wrote to Blair: 'Sadly, it is clear to us – as it is to almost the entire party and the entire country – that without an urgent change in the leadership of the party it becomes less likely that we will win the next election.' Polling evidence supported this. In May ICM had reported that Brown led the Prime Minister by 15 points as someone voters say is more likely to make them vote Labour. He had an eight-point lead over Blair as being on voters' wavelength and a 23 point lead as someone who looks to the future. The poll also showed that Labour's base of support was narrowing.

The sound of political foundations crumbling under the Prime Minister could be heard all over Westminster. The point came when Blair's survival depended on offering a timetable for his departure which would give his successor time to establish himself before the general election which must be held not later than 2010. Blair bowed to the inevitable and made his statement on a planned visit to Quinton Kynaston School in north London. But it was not the statement his Chancellor wanted. It stretched his tenure at 10 Downing Street out to the last minute possible without provoking a major revolt, it left as much doubt about precise timing as he could get away with, and it was as graceless as any announcement of resignation has ever been.

He said:

'The first thing I would like to do is to apologise, actually, on behalf of the Labour party for the last week, which with everything that is going on back here and in the world, has not been our finest hour, to be frank …

'Now, as for my timing and date of departure, I would have preferred to do this in my own way, but as has been pretty obvious from what many of my cabinet colleagues have said earlier in the week, the next party conference in a couple of weeks will be my last party conference as party leader, the TUC next week will be my last TUC, probably to the relief of both of us.

'But I am not going to set a precise date now. I don't think that's right. I will do that at a future date and I'll do it in the interests of the country and depending on the circumstances of the time.'

For Brown, it could have been worse. He had feared Blair trying to hold on until the general election was almost upon them. Instead, he now knew that the new leader would have almost three years to establish himself and win the election. But it could have been an awful lot better. He wanted an exact date to plan to, to ensure that there was no divisive battle for the leadership – the outcome he feared most, for it would make a nonsense of all his caution of the years since 1994. He would have liked private advance notice of the date, which leaders give their chosen successor, to give him a head start when it came to marshalling their forces. Clement Attlee did it for Hugh Gaitskell, Harold Wilson for Jim Callaghan, but Tony Blair did not do it for Gordon Brown. More than any of that, Brown would have liked a far shorter period between the announcement and Blair's actual departure. What Blair did was to provide almost a year in which enemies could mass their forces, rivals could emerge, and Brown's weaknesses could be examined and magnified under the harsh scrutiny directed at someone likely to be the next Prime Minister, to see if any of them can be used to ruin him. And that's how it was left. Right at the end of April 2007, Brown still did not know exactly when Blair was going to go. He had no means of trying to ensure that he took over in circumstances that would give him the best chance of succeeding.

Is that a problem? I asked Brown. He laughed, he said something non-committal, and waves of irritation seemed to be emanating from a place deep inside him where he has buried it. Later I asked one of his closest associates, who said, through gritted teeth: 'It's where we are.'

Blair had allowed plenty of time for such media events as the *Financial Times* front-page lead on 19 March 2007 quoting Lord Turnbull, Permanent Secretary to the Treasury for four years under Brown and Cabinet Secretary from 2002 to 2005, as saying Brown showed 'Stalinist ruthlessness' and treated colleagues with 'more or less complete contempt', that he had a 'very cynical view of mankind and his colleagues' and 'cannot allow them any serious discussion about priorities. His view is that it is just not worth it and 'they will get what I decide.' Most damaging of all, he said Brown had 'a Macavity quality. He is not there when there is dirty work to be done'.

It was exactly what the Blairites wanted to hear, especially the Macavity bit. Turnbull was apparently horrified to see in it the paper, thinking he was having a drink and off-the-record chat with his old journalistic chum Nicholas Timmins, and it was not a balanced report of his views. It seems odd that a man of Turnbull's experience, whose whole professional life required being careful what he said, could make such a mistake; and equally odd that a journalist like Timmins, who has good contacts in government and whose professional success relies on their trusting him, would betray Turnbull. Yet if Turnbull is right, one of these things must have happened.

Was it true of Brown, I asked Neil Kinnock? 'Meetings that go through the motions really irritate him,' he said. 'I tolerate a lot of that to get the things I want, whereas Gordon, when he starts to get bored, slams papers down, huffs and puffs. He doesn't suffer fools gladly, he's willing to let it show, not in an offensive discourteous way but makes no pretence of accepting it. People become very petty so he's disadvantaged by it. But if someone comes to him needing help, you could mistake him for his father. Or his mother.'

Kinnock insists that Blair was not behind the relentless, though pointless, efforts to find a way of stopping Brown. 'Tony resolved a long time ago that his successor would be Gordon. The bad feeling is overdone. Most of it is caused by the people around Tony and Gordon, started over at the Red Cow or whatever it's called [he's referring to Charlie Whelan's indiscretions in the Red Lion pub], and it eventually had its effect on the relationship between the principals. Later than they should have, they sat on their respective little tribelets and then we had a period of calm. It's medieval, the courtiers.'

Kinnock is an acute observer, but I suspect a mixture of loyalty and wishful thinking here. Medieval courtiers were often blamed for what the king did, it being unsafe to blame the king. There's no doubt that right up to the end of April 2007, a restless search was going on for a candidate called Notgordon Brown. (Ask 'a cabinet minister close to the Prime Minister' who he wanted to see as leader and he'd reply 'Notgordon Brown'.) While Charles Clarke was Home Secretary, he was easily the most credible candidate available, and was more than willing to give it a try. By sacking Clarke, Blair may have shot his own fox, for you can hardly run for leader if you have recently lost your job because your department botched something. There was wild talk of running Alan Milburn, and only marginally less wild talk of running Clarke's successor at the Home Office, John Reid. Eventually they settled on David Miliband, Tony Blair's chief policy adviser between 1994 and 2001 and now the Environment Secretary. He could never have won, but it might have painted Brown into a left wing corner from which escape would be hard; that has always been Brown's fear if he has to fight a Blairite for the leadership. Miliband kept saying he would not run, but you can hardly blame experienced political reporters for ignoring that, since their professional lives are full of politicians saying they will not do something the day before they do it.

By the time they launched their famous website to discuss Labour policy on 28 February 2007, those two veteran Blairites Charles Clarke and Alan Milburn must have realised that the search for Notgordon Brown was becoming forlorn. In its timing and its coded statements, the website was, as *New Statesman* political editor Martin Bright put it to me, 'an act of aggression' against Brown. Bright says that if they had done it a month earlier, it would have mattered less, but it was done just after bad polling news for Brown, while friendly journalists were being briefed that Clarke still thought he could stand against Brown and that Brown was an electoral liability.

As Bright puts it, the website was aimed at Brown's jugular. That's why Neil Kinnock rang 'my friend and comrade' Charles Clarke and spent an hour trying to persuade him not to do it. 'I said, don't do it for the party's sake, don't do it for your own sake. What surprises me about Charles is his suspension of pragmatism. If you don't like someone it doesn't matter a damn, you get on with it. Yes, there's deep resentment there somewhere. I think quite a few of them have looked inward too much in the last 10 years.' Kinnock does not know where Clarke's loathing for Brown comes from, but is sure it is post-1997. He says Brown's success as leader will depend partly on 'whether people will suspend habits built up over the last ten years and get on with governing in the interests of the country and winning the next election'.

One politician who is going to find it well nigh impossible to give up the habits of the past ten years is Peter Mandelson. Towards the end of March 2007 this arch priest of the Blairite militant tendency stepped into the fray with a demand that the new leader should 'take new Labour forward' and not 'throw away the new Labour handbook'. He said no one knew enough about Brown's intentions, and asked: 'Is he going to do it in a new Labour way … or is he going to be a more Labour Party animal?' It was code for: David Miliband is Notgordon Brown. Behind the scenes he was trying to persuade Miliband of this.

Miliband was at last forced to rule himself out in terms that no one could misunderstand in an article in the *Observer* on 22 April. The search for Notgordon Brown was over. Even the most fanatical Blairites were now forced to recognise the cruel truth that he did not exist. Brown only had to sit out the announcement from the Prime Minister. And it is a strange but certain truth that during those last days before Tony Blair's announcement of Thursday 10 May 2007 that he was going to cease to be leader and Prime Minister on 27 June, Gordon Brown had no more idea of the timetable than you or I. He had to do exactly what we did – read the newspapers, and try to guess from them what the Prime Minister's intentions were.

14

What Gordon Did

I am not an economist. When Gordon Brown talks of how he 'constructed a new monetary and fiscal regime' I only dimly understand. But I think I know what he has been striving for these last ten years. For Brown, economics are a means to an end. Like Attlee and Bevan in the 1940s, like Jimmy Maxton and Neil Kinnock, he is horrified by poverty and lack of opportunity for the poor, and believes politicians can change them. But he thinks they have to go about it patiently, pragmatically, and unhindered by rigid ideologies.

He has been the most powerful Chancellor of the 20th century, because none of his predecessors – even the immensely powerful Lloyd George, who until Brown came along was the 20th century's longest-serving Chancellor – were in as strong a position in relation to the Prime Minister. The things the Blair government has achieved or failed to achieve on the domestic front are down to Brown more than any other single person.

The record does not begin to match that of Labour's landmark government, the Attlee government of 1945–51. The comparison, made in Chapter 9, may not be entirely a fair one – the post-war mood for change gave Attlee more of a following wind in terms of public opinion than the Blair government has had – but the fact remains that in three years Attlee and his colleagues created health and education systems free at the point of use as well as Britain's first comprehensive welfare system; a contribution towards the quality of life of its poorest citizens unmatched by any other government in British history, including the present government.

Even Attlee's government got into economic trouble, as Brown points out. Apart from the Attlee government, all previous Labour governments, under Ramsay MacDonald, Harold Wilson and James Callaghan, have found themselves blown off course. Wilson's government saw some advances, especially in education; MacDonald's saw none (a point well made at the time by Jimmy Maxton, and recorded by Maxton's biographer Gordon Brown) and Callaghan's was crippled by political and economic conditions.

Attlee delivered full employment, and here the present government can match him. John Edmonds sees that as Brown's achievement: 'Blair thought this could not be done; when he rewrote Clause 4 he refused to include a reference to full employment, because he thought it would not be achievable.' Edmonds adds to Brown's achievement the development of the regions, so that the parts of the country seen as poor relations for decades are escaping from the poverty trap. 'In about 2002 the north-south divide changed, and migration from north to south started to come to an end', says Edmonds.

Britain is incomparably better at training its workforce than it was. Regional Development Agencies and the other government initiatives to promote training have come, by and large, from the Brown-led Treasury, rather than from departments responsible for industry or education.

What about the question closest to the heart of the son of the Manse, who saw poor families at his father's door, their children clearly in dire need, and went into politics partly to banish child poverty from the land – the question of poverty, and in particular child poverty? In 1997 there was a huge mountain to climb – a mountain that was climbed in the years 1945 to 1979, and now has to be climbed all over again; for the Thatcher government, in its first five years, presided over a rise in child poverty from one in nine children to one in three.

There is a clear commitment to end child poverty by 2020. But in March 2006, the government had to announce its failure to reach the first milestone – lifting one million children above the poverty line. It had, however, made progress. Kate Green, chief executive of the Child Poverty Action Group, showed that poverty campaigners appreciated that. 'We should not forget that in the last six years, 700,000 children have been lifted out of relative poverty,' she said. 'It's not enough, but without this ambitious target and the extra resources the government has committed to tackling child poverty, it's unlikely that such progress would ever have been made.'

But even David Miliband, who is not shy of claiming credit for the government, wrote in that famous *Observer* article in April 2007 where he ruled himself out as a leadership candidate: 'Child poverty has been turned round, but the gap in life chances has not been.' Gordon Brown has been a cautiously redistributive Chancellor, but very cautious, and not redistributive enough for many. The gap between rich and poor is actually wider than when New Labour came to office. If the powerful Chancellor takes credit for the government's economic successes, this startling failure must have something to do with him, too.

Brown and his Economic Secretary Ed Balls reply that they have reduced relative inequality. The incomes of the lowest-paid 20 per cent of the population are considerably nearer to the average than they were in 1979, and have grown faster than other incomes. And that's true too. But Brown and Balls accept that it is not enough.

We know, however, that one of the few changes Tony Blair blocked was Brown's wish to raise Thatcher's 40 pence in the pound top rate of income tax to 50 pence in the pound for the top 1 per cent earning over £100,000. In the end Brown and Ed Balls seem to have been less upset than you might have expected from this reverse, since they say they got more money from Stamp Duty than the income tax change would have brought them. It was, they say, a tactical and not a strategic disagreement – how best to reassure those earning £40–50,000.

Young children need, not just money and healthcare, but also education. Brown was impressed by Professor Ruth Lister's finding that the first four years of a child's life are when they learn most. Perhaps he was unfairly dismissive when he said in his Donald Dewar Memorial Lecture in October 2006: 'For fifty years, the British welfare state failed young children in our country, offering the under fives little more than the benefit of maternity services for the mother, vaccination, and then, a demand to attend school at five.' All that, after all, was light years ahead of what went before, when poor families could expect to lose at least one pre-school child to a treatable illness. But his boast of 'a transformation of services for the under fives … maternity rights, new children's benefits, reading materials, nursery schools and Sure Start and children's centres' was one of which he had a right to be proud.

If pre-school children fell to Brown, once they passed the age of five they seem to have become Blair's responsibility, except when they wanted vocational training. Brown found the money, but primary, secondary and higher education was an area on which Blair had decided views, and took advice only from his own adviser Andrew Adonis, now Lord Adonis and an education minister.

Passing remarks, from which he swiftly moves on before he can be nailed to them, suggest that Brown is not at all impressed by what Blair and Adonis have done. In a speech on 31 January 2007 he credited Microsoft's Bill Gates with the thought that 'your salary, which historically was most determined by what country you were in, in the future will be determined by … what education you've had.'

Selection at the age of 11, which Labour theoretically opposes, but which is more widespread now than it was in 1997, was referred to briefly in his Donald Dewar Memorial Lecture in October 2006: 'Today, as a society, we are far more aware of the potential of people, and of the range and diversity of that talent that was never properly picked up in IQ tests that dealt only with one type of analytical intelligence.' That is the authentic voice of the boy who was fast-tracked at the age of 11, and still believes in the ringing condemnation of the system that he wrote when he was just 15: 'I thought continually of how it could have been for these young guinea pigs, how the strain of work, the ignominy and rejection of failure could have been avoided.'

He has done more than most politicians to focus world attention on the problems of the poorest nations and of the environment, seeing the two as linked. He commissioned Sir Nicholas Stern – former Chief Economist at the World Bank and Head of the British Government Economic Service – to report on the economics of climate change. Purists could well argue that it should not take a report showing that degrading and destroying our environment actually costs us money to persuade us to stop doing it. Brown has a sufficiently cynical view of human nature to believe that he must show big business that caring for the environment is in its own interests, and Stern did that effectively.

Stern also showed, as Brown put it in a speech in New York in April 2006, that 'the risks of climate change will not be evenly spread, but will hit poorest countries most, making the issue of climate change one of justice as much as economic development. And because we have to spend $6 billion of aid simply to respond to this humanitarian crisis, resources are being diverted to tackling the short-term consequences of environmental change and away from dealing with the causes of underdevelopment and environmental neglect.'

His collection of high-profile advisers on the environment were derided as a gimmick, but such names as former US Vice President Al Gore, Microsoft's Bill Gates, Jean-Pierre Garnier of GlaxoSmithKline, Lee Scott of Wal-Mart, and Terry Leahy of Tesco, at least indicated the status in the world that Britain's Chancellor had. CBI Director-General Digby Jones thought it was 'window dressing' and that Brown might really want to do radical things of which Jones would not approve. On the other hand, War on Want said it was 'amazing' that Brown was 'willing to trumpet the fact that he is taking advice from Lee Scott, a chief executive who pays staff low wages yet earned $17.5m [£10m] in 2004'. The charity pointed out that Wal-Mart had advised its managers 'to push down medical benefits to staff and ensure trade union members were kept out of the company' and advised that when Brown met Scott, 'he could ask him whether he would advise British companies to roll out Asda Wal-Mart's anti-union policies, which recently led to the company being fined almost £1m in the north-east for offering illegal inducements to workers to disown their union'. David Miliband's April 2007 *Observer* piece seems to claim credit for the fact that people are even thinking about climate change: 'Economic stability and confidence have created the space for people to demand a greener, more ethical economy ...' This is pushing it. The government cannot claim the credit for creating the environmental lobby.

Brown is not much loved in Europe, where you hear complaints that he does not seem to take his counterparts sufficiently seriously, always arriving late for meetings of finance ministers and leaving them early. They know that he has been the stumbling-block to Britain joining the single currency. For all their resentment about Tony Blair because of his deference to President Bush, they would have liked to see Blair getting his way on this at least. European finance ministers will not have been reassured to learn in February 2006 that Alan Greenspan, former chairman of US Federal Reserve, was becoming an unpaid adviser to Brown (or rather, formally, to HM Treasury).

In January 2007 he seemed to confirm all their worst suspicions when he rejected moves to harmonise taxes across the European Union. He looked in on the monthly meeting of EU finance ministers (a meeting he often does not attend) to lecture them on the need to deregulate. It looked to them like the English Atlanticist attacking Europe.

The harmonised tax regime which the French favoured would not help Europe, but opening up competition in financial services, energy and telecoms would, he said. 'We must not allow the single market, one of the EU's greatest successes, to be overwhelmed by national champions or protectionism. In the globalised world of the 21st century the EU must work harder to open up markets and promote competition to ensure faster growth and jobs for all of the EU's citizens.' He compared EU economic success unfavourably with that of the USA.

The word in Paris was that he was very close to the new French president Nicolas Sarkozy, whom he had known when Sarkozy was Finance Minister, and who admires the USA and Britain and believes that France, unlike Britain, has failed to modernise. The two men were said to share a Thatcherite vision for Europe. But someone close to Brown has told me that this has been massively exaggerated in Paris. 'Sarkozy has been across a couple of times and they have had conversations on those occasions. I get the impression it's Sarkozy talking at Gordon and not a dialogue.' Brown, he said, had also met the socialist candidate for the French presidency, Ségolène Royal.

Nonetheless, Sarkozy would have cheered when he heard Brown's views on globalisation. Brown does not take Tony Blair's joy in trampling on his party's sacred cows, but he does enjoy facing the left with conundrums that challenge its preconceptions. In one speech, on 31 January 2007, he managed to suggest that two traditional Labour hate figures, globalisation and the *laissez-faire* economist Adam Smith, were really progressive forces which ought to adorn any socialist banner. He told the Government Leaders Forum Europe at the Scottish Parliament: 'Two centuries ago the very idea of globalisation – of a wholly interconnected economy – was anticipated by Adam Smith ... who was born in my home town of Kirkcaldy ... I happen to believe there is a common sense world view of an inclusive globalisation founded on free trade, open markets, flexibility and matched investment ... [but] there are many round the world who, seeing globalisation as unfairness, want to stop the clock, to shelter their jobs and industries, to close their borders, to insulate themselves from change. [But this] offers an illusory safety and no long term security at all.'

Yet despite all this, despite his apparent conviction that there is nothing the public sector can do which the private sector cannot do better, still, in traditional Labour circles, Gordon Brown is family, still someone whose heart is considered to be in the right place, still thought to be on the side of the working class, in a way that Blair, and increasingly those most closely associated with him, are not. The ageing chest of Michael Foot encases something like the soul of the Labour Party, and Foot, who dislikes and distrusts Blair, admires Brown, as his authorised biographer makes clear: 'Foot has a particularly good relationship with the Chancellor, Gordon Brown [whose office was run by Sue Nye, as Foot's had once been], and warmly applauded his work at the Treasury. The day after his tenth budget on 22 March 2006, Brown took a private phone call in the Treasury, conveying a cheery message of congratulation from his 92-year-old comrade.'[1]

If Foot carries the Labour Party's soul, then the soul of what they used in the 1970s to call the labour movement – the party and the trade unions – is in the care of Foot's friend and contemporary Jack Jones, who, with the possible exception of Ernest Bevin, was once the most powerful trade union leader Britain has ever known. Jones surprised me, when I spoke to him during Blair's second term, with the fervour of his support for Brown, and his conviction that the Labour government would recover its sense of purpose as soon as Brown replaced Blair. This could not happen fast enough for Jones.

The Brown inner circle these days has changed, of course, but the similarities are striking. Sue Nye is still there, organising his life and his office, and no one gets to see him without her approval. Ed Balls and Ed Miliband, brother of David, are still there, offering a huge intellectual resource to the Chancellor – 'Brown's brains' as someone put it to me – but they are now required to be public performers as well, and neither of them are top class at that. Key younger political allies include Yvette Cooper, Minister of Housing, wife of Ed Balls and daughter of former trade union leader Tony Cooper.

Charlie Whelan is long gone, a casualty of the Blair-Brown wars in which he was an enthusiastic but perhaps not very skilled partisan. In his place Brown now has a bright young civil servant called Damian

McBride, formerly the Treasury's Head of Communications. If you heard of Whelan, but you never heard of McBride, that is not an accident. Brown and Blair both learned, much later than they should have done, what professional PR practitioners know, that a press officer who is as well known as his boss is a liability. The celebrity of Peter Mandelson and Alastair Campbell in the end did Blair harm, and that of Whelan did Brown harm. McBride may be unknown to the public, but he is trusted by the economic journalists, which is what matters. We will see a cull of spin doctors in Whitehall. They will be replaced by conventional civil servants, just as Charlie Whelan's job is now done by a civil servant.

When Ed Miliband resigned in 2005 because he was a parliamentary candidate, his place as policy adviser was taken by Spencer Livermore, a young and brainy product of the London School of Economics and the Labour Party's economic research unit. Miliband returned to Brown's side as an MP. But the key adviser these days seems to be Shriti Vadera, a former banker, who took over from Geoffrey Robinson as the brains behind the development of public-private partnerships, and is also Brown's emissary to the City. She first joined the Treasury in 1999 after 14 years at a city bank. Forceful and controversial, she was the chief treasury negotiator for the public-private partnerships on the London Underground which Brown forced on Ken Livingstone – not one of Brown's finest moments.

The Brown circle is very different from the Blair circle. It's self-evidently more cerebral – Brown surrounds himself with very brainy people of all ages, from Wilf Stevenson who is three years older than Brown himself, to McBride and Livermore who are not more than 30. But by common consent they do not have the social ease of the Blair circle. They do not have the effortless gift you find in the Blair circle of making people feel important.

Right now, says a journalist who has extensive dealings with them, they feel embattled and conspiratorial. This probably reflects the position Brown is in, where anything he says, any firm policy initiative he offers, is a hostage to his enemies – but those same enemies, on the Conservative benches as well as his own, are publicly taunting him for not offering any.

In a sense, they reflect their principals. Blair is an inveterate charmer, in private and in public. Brown in public sometimes seems dark and dour, and pure intellect. In reality, he isn't. He is a man of great humour and charm, and the dense, sometimes impenetrable language he uses is not all he is capable of. He more than any other politician knows how to use words like a good journalist, making himself clear and interesting, when he wants to. He learned the skill in the rigorous training-ground of television. Sadly, the habits of a politician have taken over most of the time, and he has either forgotten the skill or does not see fit to use it often. He does not have the patience, or see the need, for 'stroking' his colleagues, building up their self-esteem. He doesn't suffer fools gladly.

He can appear like a politician without what Dennis Healey calls 'a hinterland'. But he isn't. 'Every time I see him he has a new book to recommend', an old friend tells me. He reads history, of course, but also poetry. It's not surprising that a historian enjoys the first World War poets, but a less predictable love is the 17th-century poet William Cowper, and he has a fairly recent enthusiasm for Andrew Motion. His tastes are not particularly highbrow: he reads the Scottish novelist Ian Rankin, and has read most of the Harry Potter books. He and Sarah relax in the late evenings over films, often whatever is showing on Sky. One of his less widely reported initiatives has been to help save his local football club, Raith Rovers. When its owners decided to sell the club he has supported all his life, Brown led and raised money for a £1.3 million community takeover.

He shares with Blair a set of strongly-held Christian beliefs. 'He's a practising Presbyterian, and believes in direct communication with God', says Nick Brown. But the Presbyterian faith is very different from the Catholic (or at least neo-Catholic) faith embraced by Blair. The minister is more like a Jewish rabbi – a teacher, and in no way superior to his congregation. The duty to perform public service is central to the faith of Scottish Presbyterians. As often happens in times of trouble, he turned to his faith when he lost his daughter Jennifer, and it became a far more important part of his life. 'At key personal times like marriage and baptism, Gordon is very engaged with religion – more than I'd have expected', says someone who knows him well. 'But it is still in a very private way.'

He also shares with Blair an ecumenical approach to religion – probably more so than Blair, for he has seen in Scotland the harm that religious sectarianism can do. He is close to the chief rabbi Jonathan Sachs, whom he greatly admires; they meet most months, and even have 'shiurs' – studying passages from the Torah – together. He is also close to the Scottish Catholic prelate Cardinal Keith Patrick O'Brien, and has been able to influence the Cardinal. 'Cardinal O'Brien put out a statement supporting independence for Scotland but Brown put him right and he has withdrawn from that' says the editor of the *Scottish Catholic Observer*, Harry Conroy. Brown and O'Brien launched bonds to raise money for vaccinating children in Africa, and Brown met the Pope who agreed to buy the first bond.

'He would want to know why a Sikh's a Sikh, to understand Islam or Janeism, he's built like that and he has this massive capacity for hoovering up knowledge', says Neil Kinnock. But there is a crucial difference between Brown's religiosity and Blair's, apart from the fact that Brown is a Scottish Presbyterian and Blair is almost certainly on the verge of being received into the Roman Catholic church. Brown does not wear his religion on his sleeve. His faith is the faith his father preached for 40 years, and it's deep and private. You cannot imagine him saying that he will answer to his God for his decisions. He knows who is going to judge Brown the politician. We are.

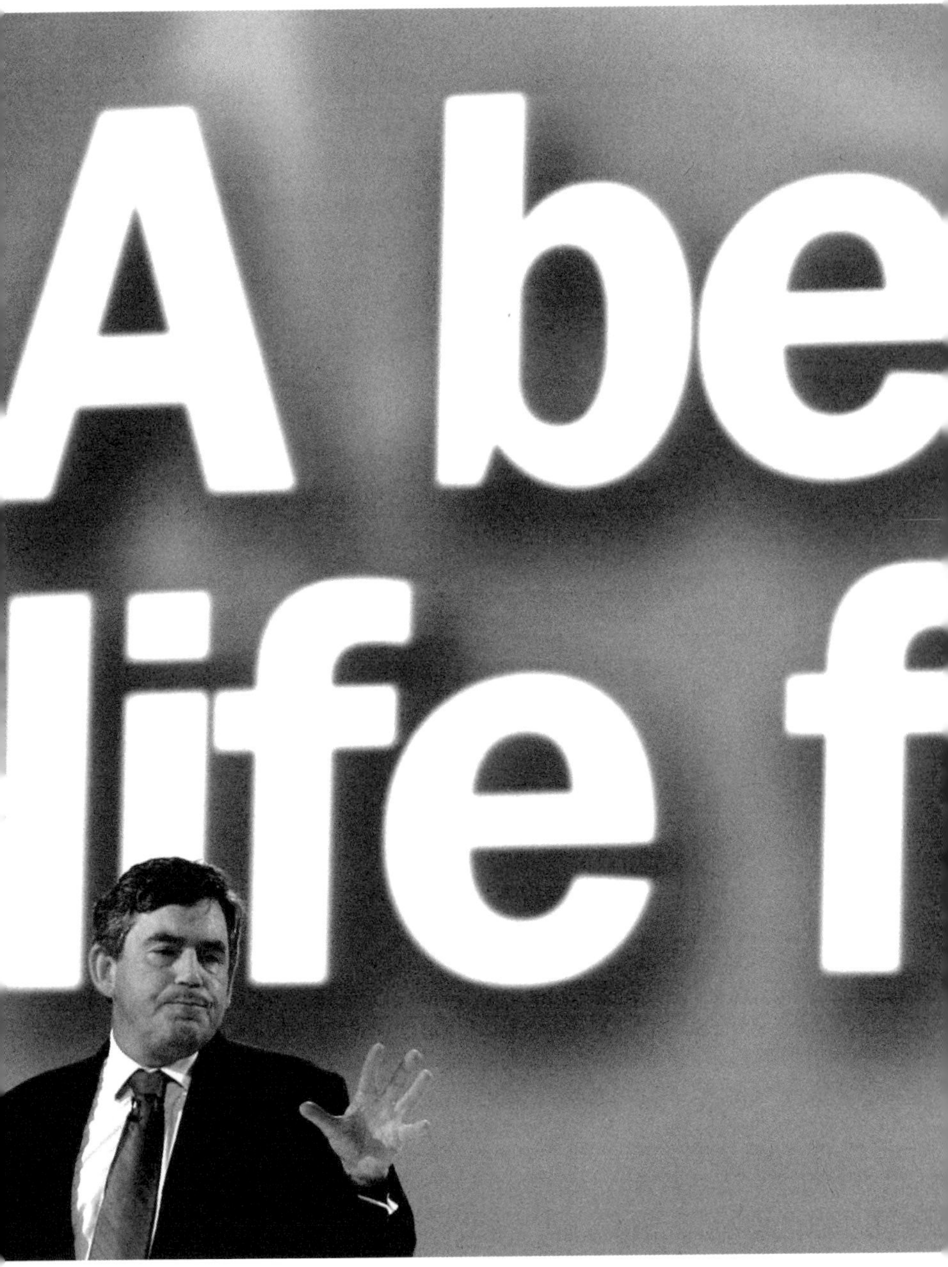
A be
life f

ter

or all

15

What Gordon Might Have Done

Politicians dislike speculating about what might have been. There are two reasons, one which does them credit, and another which is rather discreditable.

The good reason is that a practical politician looks, not to the past, but to the future. He or she is in the business of changing what can be changed, not of vain speculations about what might have been.

The discreditable reason is that the immediate past is a political minefield. Too harsh a spotlight on what a government minister has done in the past, say, ten years, nearly always exposes something nasty.

Gordon Brown thinks speculation about what would have been different if he, and not Tony Blair, had been elected to lead the Labour Party in 1994 is a waste of time, when he could be planning for what he will do when he does get to lead his party.

Brown may dislike historical 'ifs'. I enjoy them, and not just because they relieve me of the normal requirement to get facts right. There is a practical purpose. This book aims to establish, as far as possible, what sort of Prime Minister Gordon Brown will be, on the basis of what we have seen of him. Since he is playing his cards close to his chest; and since, as Macmillan said, Prime Ministers are in the hands of 'events, dear boy, events'; judging what Brown will do when he moves from Number 11 to Number 10 Downing Street is a little like walking round a maze in pitch darkness.

But looking back, it's possible to establish with some degree of confidence the occasions upon which Brown, had he been Prime Minister, would have adopted a different course from the one Blair in fact adopted. It is possible to fit that into some sort of pattern, from which we can get an idea of what sort of Prime Minister Brown might have been over the past ten years. And once we've done that, we'll be in a better position to judge what sort of Prime Minister he's actually going to be.

So it is more than just a self-indulgence for me to move, for this chapter alone, into a parallel universe. It is June 2007, and a broadsheet newspaper editor has invited me to sum up Brown's first ten years at Number 10 Downing Street, into which he moved in 1997. The sub-editor might well have put on it the headline:

'Brown must go' say modernisers

It's hard, now that he seems impregnable, to remember that before the 1997 general election, Gordon Brown's leadership of the Labour Party looked distinctly shaky.

Then as now, the so-called modernisers were discontented with him, feeling that he had squandered Labour's opportunity. Then, as now, they sigh for a Blair premiership, regretting that Brown's appetite for constitutional Labour Party reform seemed so easily sated.

Yes, he lanced the long-standing boil of Clause Four of Labour's constitution – that odd anomaly which, in theory though never in practice, committed Labour to wholesale nationalisation. But after that, he seemed to tire of the Labour Party's internal affairs. The Labour Party conference is still a policy-making body, still capable of embarrassing the leader; and any constituency Labour Party or trade union can still get its pet motion onto the annual conference agenda. This sort of anarchic procedure does not exactly give the Party a modern image, say the modernisers.

But in 1997 they looked as though they could mount a serious threat to Brown if they chose. Today, with three general election victories behind him, he is pretty well immovable.

Brown's massive 97-seat majority in June 1997 silenced his critics temporarily.

Privately, the modernisers claimed it could have been twice as big if the leader had been more identifiably from 'Middle England' rather than the strange, hirsute, left wing land beyond Hadrian's Wall. They pointed out that a family man, with a nice wife and nice children – this is all code for Tony Blair – could have won an even bigger majority. But 97 was good enough for most people.

It was enough for Brown to take a few instant decisions without too much controversy. He swiftly cancelled a now long-forgotten proposal to build a vast round shed in Greenwich, south London, which the Conservatives had planned as a symbol for the Millennium, but for which no one had thought of a use. Brown had always been sceptical about the project. The decision enraged Peter Mandelson, whose defection in 1994 had done so much to give Brown, rather than Blair, the leadership. Mandelson was rewarded – inadequately, in Mandelson's view – with the leadership of the House of Commons.

The luckiest MP in that Parliament was Michael Portillo. He hung onto his seat in 1997 by the narrowest of margins – just a handful of votes after three recounts. If the Labour majority had been any bigger, he would not have survived. And if he had failed to survive, he would have missed his best chance to stand for the vacant Tory leadership. As it was, he stood and won.

Brown's initial confidence that he could marginalise an opposition leader imprisoned by the Neanderthal right took a nasty dent when, as Opposition Leader, Portillo went soft and liberal and cuddly, every so often cheekily sniping from the left. He proved to be the Conservatives' Neil Kinnock, determined to make his Party electable again by bringing it towards the political centre.

Portillo even claimed that the battle between left and right was out of date, and talked about something called a 'Third Way'. Foreign Secretary Tony Blair was put up to attack it – a clever choice, for he was the cabinet's chief moderniser. Blair, in an uncharacteristically irritable speech, called the Third Way 'vacuous', but there was no doubting its popular appeal.

But Labour disappointed many of its supporters with a determination to stick to the Conservative government's spending plans, and its determination to finance public services through the Private Finance Initiative.

Education Secretary Anne Taylor ensured that every state school was funded at *the same level, and none was allowed to select the brightest pupils. Relying heavily on a Prime Minister who thought education in the rest of the country should be run the way it was run in his native Scotland, and whose personal childhood experience of an eleven-plus experiment in Kirkcaldy was an unrelieved misery, she announced: 'There will be no failures, and no schools designed for failures.' But, to the disappointment of the left, private schools remained untouched – a task for her successor, she said mischievously.*

Health Secretary David Blunkett tore down the health service's 'internal market', embarked on a hugely expensive modernisation programme, and grandly announced the end of health service rationing (a promise, it has to be said, which the government has not been able to keep.) Agriculture Minister Gavin Strang, with lordly disdain for the once powerful farming and landowning lobby, put himself at the head of the movement to ban foxhunting, which he had the pleasure of seeing passed into law.

Transport Secretary Ken Livingstone – Brown's bravest appointment, or his stupidest, depending on who you listen to – has enjoyed himself so much in the job that he rather disconcerted his leader by refusing to return to London politics after the massive programme of regional government. Brown had hoped he would stand for Mayor of London. Instead, the task of running London's transport, education, and taxation, went to that fine old warhorse Frank Dobson. Livingstone happily returned to what he does best, upsetting the airlines by refusing a third runway at Heathrow, upsetting the car lobby with motorway tolls, and upsetting the left by allowing public-private partnerships to bring in some capital for a partial renationalisation of the railways.

The events of 9/11 brought Brown rushing to New York to pledge solidarity with the American people, and thence to Washington to form a common front against terrorism with President George W. Bush, an alliance that led to British troops fighting alongside the Americans in Afghanistan.

But the common front started to crack as it became clear that Iraq was next on Bush's menu.

The infinitely cautious Brown would not go to war unless there was a clear post-war plan. The American president's assurance that it was enough if they just 'stop Saddam doing this shit' did not reassure him. He wanted to wait for a final report from Han Blix's weapons inspectors, though Bush told him that Blix 'wouldn't know a nuke if he was sitting on it'. Worst of all, he wanted to wait until the United Nations was willing to sanction the war. Bush despaired of the British premier, seeing him as typical of flabby Europeans.

Brown found himself at public odds with Bush (who referred to him as the leader of Old Europe) and at private odds with his own Foreign Secretary. Blair's loyalty seems to have been strained to the limit. From that moment on, a distinct group of right-wingers in the Party coalesced around the Foreign Secretary.

By the time of the American presidential election in 2004, Labour had been re-elected with a reduced majority, helped by the Americans' failure to bring about peace in Iraq, which meant that the simmering dispute in Labour's ranks did not break out into open warfare; and Brown had taken the opportunity of post-election reorganisation to demote his Foreign Secretary, leaving him in charge of education instead.

President Kerry's wafer-thin victory, which was aided by Bush's international isolation, saved the special relationship, and Brown committed troops to Kerry's new multi-national force in Iraq under the leadership of the United Nations.

Kerry's victory probably saved Brown's premiership. There are, of course, voices calling on him to go, but he enjoys good health and the respect of his Party, and the Blairites are unlikely to be able to mount an effective coup: their stance over Iraq may have been forgiven, but it has not been forgotten. And in any case, they cannot any longer be sure that their man would inherit the job. Ken Livingstone has skilfully transmogrified from Red Ken to Reliable Ken. To stage a coup against Brown would risk putting Livingstone in Downing Street. Right now it looks as though the Blairites are content to stick with nurse, for fear of finding something far, far worse.

Far-fetched? Well, yes, a little, though at each point, Brown's known views suggest he might well have acted in the way I have described, and the results I have described might well have followed. And I readily plead guilty to the charge of selecting only those events which suited my argument. This is not a scientific exercise.

The point, though, is that it really does matter who the man at the top is. The British political system gives huge power to the Prime Minister – more than to the leader in almost any other western democracy – because it gives him, within limits, control of the legislature as well as the executive. The majority party in Parliament consists of members of his own party, and of men and women whose hopes of advancement are in the Prime Minister's hands. Power in the last 30 years has become increasingly centralised on Number 10.

A Brown premiership would certainly have been different from a Blair premiership. And a Brown premiership starting in 2007 is going to be different from the Blair premiership we are used to. But how different? That is what I will try to gauge in the next chapter.

16

What Gordon's Going
to Do Next

By holding on as long as he did, Blair effectively seems to have released Brown from the requirement to be a good Blairite. And after ten years of Blair dominance, especially watching events unfold in Iraq, the British public is clearly not in the mood to respond to a promise of more of the same. This would lead to certain defeat at the next election. Brown believes he will have to offer them something different – but not too different.

It's the old dilemma revisited – the same one that he faced in 1994 and which has come back to haunt him periodically ever since, for example at the time when he could have brought Blair down over trust schools. He has to be different from Blair, but not in a way that frightens off the people who only voted Labour because they trusted Blair not to do anything which might damage the middle classes – or 'Middle England' as we are now supposed to call them.

So he will have to be different, and the consequences of that difference will affect us all. For the British political system rests so much power in its Prime Minister that the holder of the office often changes the whole course of his nation's history. If Edward Heath had beaten off Margaret Thatcher's challenge to his leadership in 1976 – and he might well have done – we would live in a very different country today, perhaps comfortably at the heart of Europe and glowering suspiciously across the Atlantic. Whether we would be better off or worse off, it's impossible to say, but our lives would certainly be different. Brown is giving as few hostages to fortune as he can, and everyone who knows him says: 'You have to remember he's a very cautious man.' Nonetheless, things will change.

David Chaytor, Labour MP for Bury, is one of the most interesting Labour MPs. He's not a serial rebel, and if promotion went on ability rather than unquestioning obedience he would be in the government. He thinks Brown is 'impressive, able to judge what's achievable, and has understood the limits of the central state'. He adds that Brown was fond of five tests – he had five tests for the Millennium Dome, and he has five tests for entry into the single currency. So Chaytor has five tests for a Brown administration. They are: will he move towards a more progressive policy on schools, climate change, health, nuclear policy, and foreign policy.

If we take a close look at the first, schools policy, we see an illustration of the dilemma Brown faces. Chaytor asks: will he get rid of selection and provide a system which gives the best education for all? Chaytor is horrified that, after ten years of a Labour government, there are still great swathes of the country, including the whole of Kent and Buckinghamshire, which select children on ability at the age of 11 – and inevitably select out the poor; and that trust schools, academies and the rest seem to presage a two-tier education system. He is pleased that Brown has left the door partly open on selection and on academies.

Brown is against selection, and his own experience of it when he was 10 is not a happy one. Conventional wisdom in Labour circles has it that a move to end it would provoke a middle-class backlash which would cost seats in places like Kent, though this seems to me distinctly unproven: the thousands of Kent children offered only secondary modern schools in Kent include members of the middle class. Still, it seems likely that Brown will be too cautious to move on this, at any rate this side of the general election. He tends to talk about how structures are less important than the personal development of children, which sounds a little like a way of saying that structures are too politically delicate to deal with. He talks of teachers moving from being lecturers to having an enabling role, about the individual development of the child, about giving the best resources to every pupil, about greater involvement by parents – not about selection.

He frequently says: 'The best economic policy is a good education policy.' On 31 January 2007 he told the Government Leaders Forum Europe at the Scottish Parliament: 'Almost 500 years ago Scotland led the world with the vision that every child in every village, every town and every city should have the right to schooling ... Lifelong education should start with the world class ambition that we raise the school leaving age to 18.' It was, he said, the next staging post in the progression. Universal education for 5–11 year olds arrived in 1893; for 5–14s in 1918; for 5–15s in 1947; and for 5–16s in 1972.

He knows that education raises passions, both inside and outside the Labour Party, which may be why he has talked less about it than about, say, health. He also knew that anything he said about education before Blair's resignation announcement would trespass on an area Blair made his own, and be interpreted as disloyalty. But Chaytor can cling to what Brown said two years ago to the Joseph Rowntree Foundation: 'It is because neither potential nor intelligence can be reduced to a single number in an IQ test – and because ability should never be seen as fixed – that no individual should be written off at 7, 11 or 16, or indeed at any time in their life.'

The journalist, former Blair aide and educational campaigner Fiona Millar had a go at extracting from Brown's speeches the sort of school system he would like to see: 'Non-selective schools with a vital part to play in supporting and revitalising communities? A focus on supporting the diversity within rather than between schools? Resources directed at individual children through a progressive funding structure? Smaller class sizes for some?' His speeches seem not entirely consistent with his support for the education bill, she says. 'What does he think of

schools with barely any democratic representation, let alone empow-
ered parents, on their founding trusts or governing bodies? Does he
really believe that spending millions on individual cutting-edge buildings is the best way of developing progressive universalism? Or would
he have rather spent that money on individual children and families
in many more schools? How can he reconcile the concept of strong
neighbourhoods with a policy that may lead to local schools being shut
down due to falling rolls and falling demand? What sort of aspiration will
children in those neighbourhoods have if secondary education ceases
to exist in their communities?'[1]

Neil Kinnock counsels caution. 'Instinctively I think he's not going to
deprive people of what they believe to be choices from this marketised
system, but I am sure he does not think the answers are there but in
continued investment for the benefit of all. He's got a strong belief in
education as the emancipator of all people. A higher level of skill makes
people more free.' But Kinnock adds: 'What he can't do and won't do is
say, I'm tearing the whole education policy up. He won't want to inflict
further disruption by putting the machine into reverse. But he's not
going to be in favour of perpetuating a selective system.'

Interestingly, however, Brown co-sponsored with Peter Lampl, the
multi-millionaire founder of the Sutton Trust, an Ipsos Mori survey on
parental aspirations, which showed that the poor start at a disadvan-
tage. Lampl is an interesting choice of collaborator, because he refused
to sponsor one of Tony Blair's academies, believing that putting a lot
of resources into a few schools was not the way to raise standards for
all.

The research found that low aspirations are inherited, which helps
to explain why, in areas with the 11-plus, the grammar schools are
largely colonised by the middle classes. 'ABs (those from managerial
and/or professional backgrounds) are three times more likely than DEs
(those from blue-collar occupational backgrounds) to say they aspired
at school to do something professional.' And 'parents with no formal

qualifications, or who (qualifications-wise) peaked at GCSE, more frequently imagine that their child will peak at GCSE or A-level, than at
degree level.'[2]

So as a long-term objective, a system offering more equality than
the one Blair and Lord Adonis have erected seems at least on the cards.
Even David Blunkett, Blair's first Education Secretary, might support
this, for he now claims to regret that he made parental ballots – by
which comprehensive education could be extended to the still-selec-
tive areas – so difficult to initiate. As Roy Hattersley put it: 'Difficult?
The rules made them impossible. Why on earth should we believe in
the integrity of a government that behaves in that way? The truth is
that Tony Blair believes in selective education, and we will not get the
English secondary system right until he goes.'[3]

It's the dilemma facing Brown wherever he looks. This is not 1997.
We have moved on, often in ways which Brown does not instinctively
like. Going into reverse is dangerous. So is not going into reverse.
That's why he's so careful what he says. He'll talk about 'new policies
to meet challenges'. He also talks, interestingly, of a new way of making
decisions, which means that he's alive to the dangers of the informal,
unminuted style of decision-making which has got Tony Blair into so
much difficulty, especially during the build-up to the Iraq war. Brown is,
in the best sense, stately. He's the sort of man who likes to see things
done properly, as his father must have been.

It also means that he likes to see the evidence. Nick Brown says:
'You will get evidence-based decision-making – Tony Blair makes the
decision, then gets the evidence.' It means that MPs will not be treated
as ciphers in quite the same way as they have become accustomed
to. Parliament will count for more. Nick Brown points out that Gordon
Brown voted for an 80 per cent elected House of Lords.

Even the Labour Party will get a look-in under Brown. Neil Kinnock,
aware of Blair's edgy relationship with his party, says: 'Gordon's very
comfortable with the Labour Party.' And he is certainly more comfortable

with the trade unions – still always an honoured guest at union func-
tions, and unlikely when he leaves office to say, as Blair did, that it is
his last TUC 'probably to the relief of both of us'. At the same time,
decisions will get made quicker, according to Wilf Stevenson, because
'there will be one source of power in Whitehall instead of two'.

Will the relationship with the USA change, as Chaytor hopes? In one
sense, it's bound to. There will be a new British Prime Minister and,
quite soon, a new president in Washington. The chemistry will change.
A lot of the transatlantic relationship depends on personal chemistry. It
has developed most successfully when the chemistry worked: Churchill
and Roosevelt, Attlee and Truman, Macmillan and both Eisenhower and
Kennedy, Thatcher and Reagan, Blair and Clinton. And it goes wrong
when either the American president feels deceived by the British Prime
Minister (Eden and Eisenhower, Major and Clinton) or when the British
Prime Minister is too deferential, as Blair has been to Bush. (There is
a Fourth Way. You can defy the president without doing harm, so long
as you do not deceive him, as Wilson showed with Johnson over the
Vietnam war.)

Brown will need to signal a different and less deferential relationship with the USA. That's widely recognised, even by Blair's strongest
supporters. One of the key intellectual founders of New Labour, the
academic Antony Giddens, writes:

> 'In my view, [Brown] must seek an opportunity to show independ-
> ence of mind from the current US regime … I have been a consist-
> ent supporter of Tony Blair and still regard him as an outstanding
> leader. But I don't understand why … he put all his eggs in the Bush
> basket. Blair from the beginning has supported multilateralism in
> world affairs, and made this perfectly clear in his speeches. Yet the
> Bush administration announced from the beginning that they were
> not going to hold to some of the main international agreements.
> The new US National Security Doctrine explicitly argued that Ameri-

ca's interests should be put ahead of all other considerations. Condoleeza Rice, the Foreign Secretary, spoke derisorily of "the illusory international community". The Bushites rarely missed an opportunity to run down the UN. All of this happened well before 9/11.'[4]

I have never known a time when America was so unpopular in Britain. Just after the Iraq war I recall attending an evening of stand-up comedy in a packed London pub. One comedian began his set: 'I hate Americans.' The clapping and cheering went on for several minutes, and (though he wasn't, as it turned out, a particularly good comic) he couldn't do anything wrong after that.

This is partly due to President Bush, but my sense of it is that it has much more to do with a feeling almost of national humiliation at the way our Prime Minister fawns on him. 'Yo Blair' was the moment when it crystallised. If only for domestic political reasons, Brown will need to show independence from the USA. I feel confident this will happen. Brown, as we keep saying, is a cautious man who will not want to put all his eggs in one basket. He will be able, as Neil Kinnock pointed out to me, to do this without serious difficulty because no one in their right mind can say he is anti-American. 'What we are going to see in his premiership is a willingness to be discriminating about his relationship with the White House and that will come because he is in a position of strength', says Kinnock. 'I could never comprehend the admiration Tony developed for George Bush.'

The crunch moment for Brown could come very fast. Giddens thinks it possible that 'in its dog days the Bush administration might decide to bomb the nuclear installations in Iran. The Israeli leadership could opt to do so before a new American President comes on the scene.' If that were to happen, what would Brown do? He could do no better than to signal the change of attitude by an immediate and ringing denunciation of the bombing. I would cheer him, but much more significantly, so would Anthony Giddens. It is unlikely that David Cameron could attack him for doing it (though some of his own side might), because it would be very popular. But even if Bush does not decide to pull the temple down on his way out, Brown's first task will be to extricate himself from the mess in Iraq, with as much honour and dignity and as little damage as possible. He sees that some sort of agreement with Iraq's neighbours, including Iran, is the only way forward, and I think he has the nerve to pursue this course even while Bush is still president.

His instinct, as several people close to him have suggested to me, will be to build overseas alliances wherever he can, wherever he finds a common interest. What does that mean for Britain in Europe? Brown is not what they call in Brussels 'a good European'. He has not shown enthusiasm for the European Union. He frustrated Blair's wish to be the Prime Minister who joined the single currency. 'We have all found that European economic integration had been superseded by the reality of global economic integration', he said in his Hugo Young Memorial Lecture on 13 December 2005.

> 'For fifty years we had been thinking of a world in which national flows of capital would be superseded by European flows, national sourcing of goods by European sourcing, national companies by European companies, national brands by European brands.
>
> 'But now we find ourselves in a world where national and European flows of capital are superseded by global flows, European sourcing by global sourcing, European companies and brands by global companies and brands.
>
> 'While in 1945 the greatest challenge was to build peace in Europe, in 2005 the greatest challenge is globalisation, and how to achieve social justice on a global scale.
>
> 'Asia is now producing more manufactured exports than Europe. In little more than a decade 5 million jobs will be outsourced – the biggest restructuring of the global economy since the industrial revolution.'

It is not far away from the current UKIP line – that the EU stops European countries reacting to globalisation.

But of course – like most of his speeches – this is not a policy prescription, but background thinking to policy. Brown has neither the narrow nationalism nor the single-minded Atlanticism of the Thatcherites. Prime Minister Brown will be seeking a range of allies in the world to replace the single relationship with the USA on which Blair's foreign policy was ultimately based, and many of these will be found in Europe. His argument against joining the single currency were – I think genuinely – economic and not political ones, and his objection will disappear if he is sure it will have no harmful effect on the British economy.

For a strong economy has been, and will remain, Brown's first concern. So will he, now Blair is no longer there to stop him, raise the top rate of tax from 40 to 50 pence in the pound for those earning over, say, £100,000 a year? Not in this Parliament, anyway; there is a manifesto commitment not to do it, and even though it was given against his wishes, he will not break it. That would send out exactly the signal to the voters which he has struggled so hard to avoid, and the dreaded if meaningless slogan 'tax and spend' would rise from the ashes and, he thinks, ensure he was driven out at the next election. And what if he is re-elected? He will certainly come under pressure to give the same pledge Labour gave last time, and my guess is that he might give it, calculating that the additional revenue it would produce is not so great as to take the political risk involved in leaving the door open.

Brown supporters have high hopes of a different atmosphere from Number 10. 'The key difference,' says Nick Brown, 'will be more focus on helping the disadvantaged, and less on choice.' John Edmonds says: 'We're now in a post-industrial economy and we will have to move to a pre-environmental economy. Blair just wants an economy where people can make money. For Blair the test of the economy is the opportunity for people to be entrepreneurial and make money. For Brown the test is how it can supply skills for the economy in 2050.'

Edmonds hopes for more vocational training: 'Brown has a much more egalitarian attitude to education and training than Blair and is less dewy-eyed about the rich. He may use the unions to put pressure on the employers to get more training done. He once told the CBI and the TUC to come up with solutions. The TUC said yes but the CBI said no and went to Blair. Brown might see the TUC and the unions as a useful means of raising training.'

Hopes that the New Labour obsession with marketising everything will diminish under Brown rest largely on his resistance to further marketisation of the National Health Service. According to Robert Peston, writing in 2005, Brown wants to limit the private sector to filling gaps in the capacity of the NHS, and opposes Blair's plan that the private sector should be a provider of core services to the NHS, in competition with public sector providers. It's much the same argument as the one in education: Brown fears the creation of a two-tier health service, with those on low incomes having access only to a very basic service.[5]

Brown's speeches bear this out to some extent. Two years earlier, in February 2003, he was telling the Social Market Foundation in a speech delivered at Cass Business School:

> 'In the 1980s there was an attempt – some of it largely successful, as in utilities, and some of it unsuccessful, as in health – to withdraw the state from areas where previously the public interest was seen to be equated with public ownership.
>
> 'With the consumer unable – as in a conventional market – to seek out the best product at the lowest price, and information gaps that cannot – even over the long term – be satisfactorily bridged, the results of a market failure for the patient can be long-term, catastrophic and irreversible. So even if there are risks of state failure, there is a clear market failure.'

The case for a comprehensive national insurance policy, he said, was 'greater now than in 1948 when the scientific and technological limitations of medicine were such that high cost interventions were rare or very rare – there was no chemotherapy for cancer, cardiac surgery was in its infancy, intensive care barely existed, hip and knee replacement was almost unknown.' Today, 'the standard of technology and treatment is such that unlike 1948 some illnesses or injuries could cost £20,000, £50,000 or even £100,000 to treat and cure and ... because the costs of treatment and of drugs are now much higher than ever, and the risks to family finances much greater than ever – not just for poorer families but for comfortably off families up the income scale – the need for comprehensive insurance cover of health care is much stronger than ever ...

> 'The many market failures in health care, if taken individually, challenge the adequacy of markets to provide efficient market solutions. But what could happen when these market failures ... combine with a policy that puts profit maximisation by hospitals at the centre of health care?
>
> 'It is then that the consumer, the patient, would be at greatest risk of being overcharged, given inappropriate treatments for financial rather than medical reasons, offered care not on the basis of clinical need but on the basis of ability to pay with some paying for care they do not need and others being unable to afford care they do need – as a two-tier health care system developed.'

As in health, so in higher education – but here the message, given in the same speech, is less clear: 'Our universities operate in an increasingly global marketplace and at the same time their excellence depends upon drawing upon the widest pool of talent – making change inevitable and necessary. And one of the central questions round the world is the extent to which universities should become, in effect, the seller, setting their own price for their service, and the prospective graduate the buyer of higher education at the going rate, whether through an up front or deferred system of payment, and what are the consequences for equity and efficiency as well as choice of such arrangements.'

Universities as 'the seller, setting their own price for their services' and our 18-year-olds as 'the buyer … at the going rate' is not a cheering idea. I cling to the idea that he's clearly not convinced by it. He tries hard not to be doctrinaire about markets – though observers of his handling of the London Underground might find this hard to believe. In the same lecture he dealt with them more generally:

'Of course some on the right have argued that because market exchanges are freely entered into, markets define freedom; and the left have often slipped into arguing that because markets cannot cope with their social consequences, they are a threat to equality, liberty and the realisation of human potential; but both left and right say that for them markets or the public sector are means not ends …

'Too often, in Britain, unlike America, opportunities to start a business have seemed accessible mainly to a closed circle of the privileged … In the poorest areas in Britain where only one business is created for every six in the wealthier areas, and where not only family savings but also bank capital at the right price is often una-vailable even where men and women show initiative and dynamism, our whole approach must radically change …

'We had to come to terms with and accept the privatisation of tel-ecoms. We saw that with the right framework – regulation only where necessary and light touch wherever possible – we could create the conditions in which markets could work in the public interest and deliver choice, efficiency and a fair deal for consumers.'

Of course the leading apostle of markets was his fellow son of Kirk-caldy Adam Smith. In his Donald Dewar Memorial Lecture in October

2006 *Reinterpreting Adam Smith*, Brown the historian set out to rescue Smith from the embrace of the political right.

'Adam Smith always believed his most important book was not the *Wealth of Nations* but the *Theory of Moral Sentiments*, the book he was revising at the time of his death. "All for ourselves and nothing for other people" is a "vile maxim" he wrote, emphasising in his *Theory of Moral Sentiments* the helping hand of individuals supporting other individuals as complementary to the "invisible hand" of his *Wealth of Nations*.

'Of course, Smith and the Enlightenment writers wanted people freed from the shackles of obedience to monarchs, vested interests and all arbitrary power. That was why they called for an end to state mercantilism, and why Smith identified free markets, and the division of labour, and its specialisation, as the route to trade and prosperity.

'But while he wanted to remove these arbitrary constraints on citizens, he did not seek to remove all social bonds. The truth is that he wanted people freed from the old commands of the state, but civic responsibilities were a very different matter. Total freedom from them could diminish freedom. Civic duty mattered "whenever we feel the fate of others is our personal responsibility, we are less likely to stand idly by," he wrote.'

This is Brown the philosopher king, the first one to take up residence in 10 Downing Street since Harold Macmillan; the Brown who knows his historians and his philosophers, who brings this to every problem he expects to face in government. This is Brown the thinker, sometimes contrasted with Blair the man of action. Perhaps a thinker in power is preferable to a man of action. If I just say, very quietly and I promise for the last time, the word Iraq, perhaps you will know what I mean. Otherwise this, from the same speech, may help:

'Out of the practice of toleration came the pursuit of liberty. And it was the battle for freedom from the old, from ancient hierarchical obligations – from the arbitrary rule of kings, from the overbearing power of bishops, from an wasteful mercantilism – that inspired 17th, 18th and 19th century philosophers from Locke to Adam Smith and then to John Stuart Mill. "The civil wars of Rome ended in slavery and those of the English in liberty," Voltaire wrote. "The English are the only people upon earth who have been able to pre-scribe limits to the power of Kings by resisting them." And he added, "the English are jealous not only of their own liberty but even of that of other nations."

'So powerful did the British idea of liberty become that – perhaps ironically – the American war of independence was fought by both sides "in the name of British liberty".

For those who think Brown has forgotten the market, there is his strong support of PFIs. And for those who think he has forgotten the traditions of his party, there is this, from his Hugo Young Memorial Lecture on 13 December 2005:

'Charities can and do achieve great transformative changes, but no matter how benevolent, they cannot, ultimately, guarantee fairness to all. Markets can and do generate great wealth, but no matter how dynamic, they cannot guarantee fairness to all. Individuals can be and are very generous but by its nature personal giving is sporadic and often conditional.

'So fairness can be advanced by but cannot, in the end, be guaranteed by charities, however benevolent, by markets, however dynamic, or by individuals, however well meaning, but guaranteed only by enabling government.'

There is an echo of Attlee here, for Attlee wrote: 'A right established by law, such as that to an old age pension, is less galling than an allowance made by a rich man to a poor one, depending on his view of the recipient's character, and terminable at his caprice.' There is reassurance here that Brown has not forgotten or rejected the traditions and purpose of his party.

Brown will take decisions in a radically different way from the one we have become accustomed to in the past ten years. We will see an end to decisions taken informally on the Downing Street sofa. Brown will run a new look government, a new style of doing government business. There will be a stronger role for Parliament, which will have the power to declare war or prevent war.

Expect a younger cabinet. The old Blair/Brown divisions are less entrenched among younger MPs. Labour politicians of Brown's generation who have been around since 1983 – Charles Clarke, John Reid – have their souls ineradicably scarred with the Blair/Brown wars. Younger politicians – the Miliband brothers, for example – may be aligned, David Miliband with Blair and his brother Ed with Brown, but they recognise that this is more of a historical accident than anything else. It doesn't mean much to them.

Brown has a new book coming out in summer 2007. Unusually for a top politician, he found the time to write it himself. He had some help from a researcher, mostly for fact-checking, but the ideas and the words are all his. It consists of essays about eight people whose lives demonstrate courage, from Nelson Mandela to Raul Wallenberg, who saved thousands of Jews from Hitler.

His writing style has declined since Maxton. Politics often does that to people. The great, shapeless papers a top politician has to read, combined with the requirement to weigh words so as not to give hostages to fortune, do not make for pithy, elegant writing. He uses words like building blocks, placing them on top of each other efficiently but without elegance. Nonetheless, it tells you something about the man.

'I remember being given, when I was ten, an encyclopaedia of twentieth century history. In it were recorded great deeds: the daring of Shackleton, the sheer determination and inspired improvisation that took his expedition across the Antarctic; the bravery and ill-fated amateurism of the Mallory and Irvine attempt on Everest in 1924; Scott's expedition to the South Pole in 1912, and Captain Oates and his last sacrifice. All of them I admired, but the page I turned to again and again was the one that surprised me most: the story – and picture – of Nurse Edith Cavell.'

Though *Courage* is not a book about Brown's policies, or even his political philosophy, there is one very tangible pointer in it to something I believe we can confidently expect from a Brown premiership. Only one of his eight character studies is still politically active – and still needing political support from the British government: Aung San Suu Kyi, the elected leader of the Burmese people, kept under house arrest by a particularly brutal military dictatorship.

Brown met her husband, Professor Michael Aris, at a Labour Party conference in the early 1990s. Only then did he realise the scale of the sacrifice she was making. 'Michael Aris told me he had not seen his wife for years, that even phone calls were becoming increasingly difficult, and that she had not seen her children for many years either.' She is the daughter of Aung San, whom Clement Attlee identified as the man on whom an independent Burma would rely; but Aung San was assassinated in 1947.

The key point is this. Gordon Brown is not just another writer, telling a story of courage and idealism. He is the Prime Minister, and he can do something. He is cautious, he weighs every word, every gesture. So when he chooses to write about Aung San Suu Kyi, you would guess that he has thought seriously about what implications will be drawn for a Brown government.

And you would be right. He has. He knows there are policy obligations arising from what he has written, and he means to honour them. I do not know exactly how he will honour them, and he will not say, but the gang of thugs who control Burma, and who have so far been able to rely on the eyes of the western world being transfixed by the Middle East, are likely soon to find that a new British Prime Minister is taking an unwelcome interest in their affairs.

The longest chapter of the book is about Nelson Mandela, for whom Brown says he has both affection and reverence, and who helped inspire him to write the book. There is also Raul Wallenberg, a Swedish business-man who during the war engineered the escape of 100,000 Hungarian Jews. Others are less obvious. Cecily Saunders, founder of the modern hospice movement, is in the book because 'she fought entrenched pro-fessional ignorance and indifference to the needs of the dying'.

To me the most unexpected and the most interesting choice is Robert Kennedy. Though no doubt a brave man, you might not expect Kennedy to be among eight exemplars of courage. Kennedy was one of the heroes of the Sixties generation, and he did come out against the Vietnam War. But he did it rather late, some of us felt: our hero might have been Senator Eugene McCarthy, who was with us all along and whose political career is now defined by his principled opposition to the war. But when you read the chapter on Kennedy, you realise that he has been chosen because he is Brown's sort of politician:

'Kennedy started to allege that Johnson had departed from his brother's policy of self-determination for the Vietnamese and that he had switched from one point of view to another. Johnson, he now believed, had Americanised the war. Once the US had waged war, he claimed, because the South Vietnamese had wanted the war. Now from that standpoint, Kennedy challenged the whole basis of the war, questioning the morality of intervention and the accuracy of the domino theory. He broke from the established view that if Vietnam fell so would the whole of Asia.

'But when Kennedy finally broke publicly with Johnson and announced his bid for the presidency in March 1968, he had a mountain to climb. He knew that part of his political challenge was to energise newly enfranchised black voters and to win back the young, anti-war Democrats who had abandoned him for Senator Eugene McCarthy – an earlier, passionate and more consistent opponent of Vietnam. But, unlike McCarthy's, Kennedy's was no protest campaign; he intended to win.'

And there, if you like, is the essence of Gordon Brown. Protest does not interest him. Winning does.

The fact that *Courage* comes out the summer Brown becomes Prime Minister is an accident. It is not a PR strategy. The writing of the book began with the death of his 10-day-old daughter Jennifer in 2002. He wanted to do something to raise money for the charity set up in her name (all the royalties from the book will go to it); and according to one of his friends, writing it was also a form of therapy.

It would not be a very good PR strategy. It plays to all the perceptions of Brown that he is trying to shake off. It makes him sound unremittingly serious, sententious, and worthy. It will not help him win the next election. There is time, he might say with Sir Francis Drake, to publish *Courage* and win the election too. But is the next general election winnable?

Brown's nightmare is being what Peter Hennessy calls a suffix Prime Minister, whose term is tacked onto the end of someone else's, as Douglas-Home was to Macmillan and Callaghan was to Wilson. He has to win the next election. The precedent he likes to remember is that of Macmillan, who took over in mid-parliament from Anthony Eden at a time when the polls looked terrible, and Eden had just taken the country into an unpopular and utterly unsuccessful war, the 1956 Suez adventure. Macmillan, taking over in January 1957, had less than three years to turn them round. He succeeded, and led his Party to victory in

1959, much to the disgust of the Revd. John Brown of Kirkcaldy. Today, the Revd. Brown's son finds that a rather comforting precedent to look back upon.

Just as they did for Macmillan in 1957, the polls are looking bad for Brown. But one of his advisers told me: 'We feel optimistic about the polls. Cameron has to persuade a lot of people who voted Labour or Lib Dem last time to vote Conservative. There is not a lot of switching going on. We have to bring the don't knows back to Labour. Why have they gone to being don't knows? My sense is that they contain people who think Gordon Brown might be a dangerous change, and others who think he is too like Tony Blair.'

He will be told he has an image problem. He will be wise not to worry too much about that. Neil Kinnock was told he had an image problem, and that he had to create for himself an entirely new and different persona; and it was a disaster. Human beings cannot do that effectively, and sensible PR people do not ask them to do it. Tony Blair was elected leader precisely because his natural persona was the image that politicians and their spin doctors believed the voters wanted. Brown cannot be Blair, and should not try. He does not need a makeover, and will, I expect and hope, resist all offers to give him one.

While reassuring the middle classes, he has to give natural Labour voters – not socialist ideologues, but people whose natural inclination is to support the poor and powerless against the plutocratic and powerful – something to revive their enthusiasm. Elections require foot soldiers, and Brown will need footsoldiers.

It is the old Brown dilemma in a new form. He must be Tony Blair and Nottony Blair, at one and the same time. He must be the left-winger who will put right the wrongs of the Blair era, and the Blairite who will not do anything that nice Mr Blair would not have done. It is not easy. But if there is a politician in Britain who can pull it off, it is Gordon Brown.

Notes

Chapter 1: A Serious Son of the Manse

1. *The Times*, 20 Feb. 1951.
2. Tom Bower, *Gordon Brown* (HarperCollins: 2004).
3. Robert Peston, *Brown's Britain* (Short Books: 2005).
4. Paul Routledge, *Gordon Brown* (Simon and Schuster: 1998).
5. Routledge, *Gordon Brown*.
6. Bower, *Gordon Brown*.

Chapter 2: The Reluctant Student Politician

1. Hugh Pym and Nick Kochan, *Gordon Brown, The First Year in Power* (Bloomsbury: 1998).
2. Routledge, *Gordon Brown*.
3. William Keegan, *The Prudence of Mr Gordon Brown* (Wiley: 2004).
4. http://www.archives.lib.ed.ac.uk/gallery/brown.shtml

Chapter 3: The Greasy Pole of Scottish Labour Politics

1. Bower, *Gordon Brown*.

Chapter 4: Between the Devil and the STV

1. Martin Westlake, *Kinnock, the Biography* (Little Brown: 2001).
2. Kenneth O Morgan, *Michael Foot, a life* (Harper Press: 2007).

Chapter 6: The Next Prime Minister?

1. Francis Beckett and David Hencke, *The Survivor* (Aurum: 2005).

2. Bryan Gould, *Goodbye to All That* (Macmillan: 1995).
3. Beckett and Hencke, *The Survivor*.
4. Bower, *Gordon Brown*.

Chapter 7: Deal or No Deal?

1. Routledge, *Gordon Brown*.
2. Pym and Kochan, *Gordon Brown, The First Year in Power*.
3. Pym and Kochan, *Gordon Brown, The First Year in Power*.

Chapter 8: The New Chancellor

1. Pym and Kochan, *Gordon Brown, The First Year in Power*.
2. Keegan, *The Prudence of Gordon Brown*.
3. Beckett and Hencke, *The Survivor*.

Chapter 10: Prudent to a Fault

1. Geoffrey Robinson, *The Unconventional Minister – My Life inside New Labour* (Penguin: 2001).
2. *Daily Telegraph*, 5 Apr. 2007.
3. Keegan, *The Prudence of Gordon Brown*.
4. *The London Review of Books*, 27 Feb. 1999.
5. Michael Mainelli, PFI *and* PPP: *Could They Result in Enron* UK? (MCB University Press: 2003).
6. *The Guardian*, 11 Jul. 2001.

Chapter 11: The Tony and Gordon Show

1. *The Times*, 19 Jan. 1998.
2. Morgan, *Michael Foot*.
3. 'Blair, The Inside Story', BBC2, Apr. 2007.
4. Peston, *Brown's Britain*.
5. *The Guardian*, 28 Jan. 2004.
6. *The Guardian*, 28 Jan. 2004.

Chapter 12: The End of the Tony and Gordon Show

1. Peston, *Brown's Britain*.

Chapter 13: The Search for Notgordon Brown

1. Ned Temko and Gaby Hinsliff, *The Observer*, 1 Jan. 2006.
2. Ned Temko and Gaby Hinsliff, *The Guardian*, 19 Feb. 2006.

Chapter 14: What Gordon Did

1. Morgan, *Michael Foot*.

Chapter 16: What Gordon's Going to Do Next

1. Fiona Millar, *The Guardian*, 14 Mar. 2006.
2. Research conducted in 2006 by Ipsos MORI on behalf of the Sutton Trust and HM Treasury.
3. Roy Hattersley, *The Guardian*, 8 Jan. 2007.
4. Anthony Giddens, *Over To You, Mr Brown – How Labour Can Win Again* (Polity Press: 2007).
5. Peston, *Brown's Britain*.

Further Reading

There are four earlier biographies of Gordon Brown. Paul Routledge's *Gordon Brown – The Biography* (Simon and Schuster: 1998) had Brown's cooperation, and is admiring, clear, and racily written – as good a guide to Brown's life before he went into government as you'll find. William Keegan's dense, informative, deeply knowledgeable *The Prudence of Mr Gordon Brown* (Wiley: 2004) concentrates a fierce beam on Brown's economic policies. Keegan, a widely respected economic commentator, likes and admires Brown but is very critical of his performance as Chancellor, believing that he has been far too cautious. The most recent, Robert Peston's *Brown's Britain* (Short Books: 2005), is obviously written by an admirer, though not an uncritical one. I owe several insights to this clear, thoughtful and penetrating book. On the other hand, Tom Bower's *Gordon Brown* (Harper Collins: 2004) reads like the splenetic ramblings of an elderly colonel in his armchair at the Athenaeum who suspects Brown of being a closet communist. Taxation, in the Bower lexicon, is always 'penal', and trade unions always 'thuggish'.

Gordon Brown, The First Year in Power (Bloomsbury: 1998) by Hugh Pym and Nick Kochan is a clear, interesting, accessible guide to a crucial year in modern political history, and offers a great deal of the personal and political, within its very limited timescale.

There are many books about Tony Blair. In my entirely unbiased opinion the best (and certainly the least friendly) is *The Survivor – Tony Blair in Peace and War* (Aurum: 2005) by Francis Beckett and David Hencke – it is the updated paperback version of *The Blairs and*

Their Court by the same authors. John Rentoul's updated *Tony Blair – Prime Minister* (Time Warner: 2002) is excellent, clear and comprehensive. *Tony Blair* by Philip Stephens (Viking: 2004) was written for the American market, so it is rather bland and uncritical, as also is Jon Sopel's much earlier book, *Tony Blair – The Moderniser* (Bantam: 1995). Anthony Seldon's huge slab of a book, *Blair*, has some interesting insights into some of Blair's colleagues, but does not work as biography.

Blair and Brown together are the subjects of Andrew Rawnsley's *Servants of the People* (Hamish Hamilton: 2000). John Kampfner's *Blair's Wars* (The Free Press: 2003) is a masterly explanation of the approach to foreign policy which Brown will inherit, and Peter Riddell's *Hug Them Close* (Politicos: 2003) on the transatlantic relationship, is very useful too. The story of the decision to go to war in Iraq is told in credible detail by Robin Cook in *Point of Departure* (Simon and Schuster: 2003).

Of Gordon Brown's own prolific writing, I recommend two books. *Maxton* (Mainstream: 1986) is key to understanding where Brown comes from politically, as well as being quite a good biography in its own right. And his own speeches are key to understanding where he is going, though they are not that accessible and make little concession to the reader in a hurry. They are published in a convenient volume, *Gordon Brown – Speeches* 1997–2006, edited and with a commentary by Wilf Stevenson as well as endorsements from some famous names, but you can find most of the speeches on the Treasury website.

Understanding New Labour election tactics is key to understanding Brown. I recommend *Campaign 1997 – How the General Election was Won and Lost* by Nicholas Jones (Indigo: 1997), and any of the other splendid books by this writer about New Labour spin; and, for the professional pollster's angle, *Explaining Labour's Landslide* by Robert Worcester and Roger Mortimore (Politicos: 1999).

Better or Worse by Polly Toynbee and David Walker (Bloomsbury: 2005) offers a well-informed analysis of New Labour's domestic record, and *Over to you Gordon* by Anthony Giddens (Polity Press: 2007) plausibly describes one way a Brown government could go.

Biographies, autobiographies and memoirs of other players which I have found useful include *Alastair Campbell* by Peter Oborne and Simon Walters (Aurum: 2004); *Who Goes Home* by Roy Hattersley (Little, Brown: 1995); *John Smith, A Life* by Mark Stuart (Politicos: 2002); *John Smith, A Life* by Andy McSmith (Mandarin: 1994); *Mandy: The Unauthorised Biography of Peter Mandelson* by Paul Routledge (Simon & Schuster: 1999); *Mandelson* by Donald Macintyre (Harper Collins: 2000); *Kinnock, The Biography*, by Martin Westlake (Little, Brown: 2001); *Charles Kennedy, A Tragic Flaw* by Greg Hurst (Politicos: 2006); *Guilty by Suspicion* by Jimmy Allison and Harry Conroy (Argyll Press: 1995); *Goodbye to all that* by Bryan Gould (Macmillan: 1995); *Off Whitehall* by Derek Scott (I.B. Tauris: 2004); *The Unconventional Minister* by Geoffrey Robinson (Michael Joseph: 2000); and *The Paymaster – Geoffrey Robinson, Maxwell and New Labour* by Tom Bower (Simon and Schuster: 2001).

Index

BEVAN

by Francis Beckett

£9.99

978-1-904341-63-5 (pb)

'I tell you, it's the Labour Party or nothing!' said Nye Bevan to his wife, Jennie Lee, in 1931. That is the key to the politician Bevan was, say Clare Beckett and Francis Beckett in their biography of the man who more than anyone instituted Britain's welfare state. Personality politics were not Bevan's politics. He was a rebel, but a reluctant rebel. That may have saved Bevan from the kind of eventual isolation that is often the lot of natural, charismatic rebels. Perhaps it also lost him the chance to lead the Labour Party: when it came to it, Bevan was not ready enough to intrigue on behalf of himself.

He was a miner's son who became a miner himself, who saw his father die in his arms with his lungs full of coal dust, who knew exactly what poverty and powerlessness meant. These were scarring, driving experiences. He was also an astringent critic of much that smacked to him of accommodation and compromise in the Labour Party. He managed to get himself expelled from the Party once, and came near to it a second time, a considerable achievement for a reluctant rebel.

Perhaps he alienated colleagues by having what Denis Healey famously called 'a hinterland' – dimensions to his personal life that were not strictly political. In politics, such dimensions are liable to evoke suspicion. In 1945 the new Prime Minister Clement Atlee 'gave Bevan a real job to do and he did it brilliantly,' say his biographers. The result was planned local authority housing and the National Health Service.

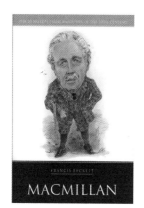

MACMILLAN

by Francis Beckett

£9.99

978-1-904950-66-0 (pb)

Macmillan (Harold Macmillan, 1894–1986, earl of Stockton 1984) Conservative politician, prime minister 1957–63. He repaired the rift between the USA and Britain created by Suez and secured for Britain co-operation on issues of nuclear defence. Paradoxically his success with the USA jeopardised his efforts to get Britain into the European Economic Community, for it was one of the reasons why de Gaulle vetoed Britain's application to join in 1963. After early successes at home as well as abroad (he acquired the nickname 'Supermac'), his party was returned with an increased majority in 1959. The later years of his administration were clouded by economic troubles, the EC veto and the Profumo scandal. But it was ill-health which caused him to resign in 1963.

THE 20 BRITISH PRIME MINISTERS
OF THE 20TH CENTURY
Francis Beckett, Commissioning Editor

Boxed Set
£175
(all 20 books plus
**TIMELINE OF THE
20TH CENTURY**
only available
as part of the set)
978-1-904950-53-0

Picture Sources

Page vi – Gordon Brown at the launch of the Labour campaign for the Dunfermline and West Fife by-election, 2006. (Courtesy of Getty Images)

Page 26 Gordon Brown in 1977 as Labour PPC for South Edinburgh (courtesy of Topfoto)

Page 54 – Brown with former Labour leader Neil Kinnock at Westminster Abbey for the Thanksgiving service for John Smith, 1994 (Courtesy of Topfoto)

Page 62 – Brown with Tony Blair and Margaret Beckett, April 1997 (Courtesy of Getty Images)

Pages 76–77 – Gordon Brown with (from left to right) Peter Mandelson, Margaret Beckett, Alistair Campbell and Tony Blair during the 1997 election campaign. (Courtesy of Getty Images)

Pages 90–91 – Leaving number 11 Downing Street to present the budget to parliament. (Courtesy of Getty Images)

Pages 202–03 – Brown with his adviser Ed Balls, December 2003. (Courtesy of Getty Images)

Pages 116–17 – Leaving Downing Street on his way to parliament to present his ninth annual budget. (Courtesy of Getty Images)

Page 132 – Blair and Brown in opposition less than a month before the 1997 election victory. (Courtesy of Getty Images)

Pages 146–47 – Brown and Blair at the Labour Party Conference in 2005. (Courtesy of Getty Images)

Pages 156–57 Gordon Brown. (Courtesy of Getty Images)

Pages 172–173 – Brown at a Press conference before the 2005 general election with Tony Blair, John Prescott and Patricia Hewitt. (Courtesy of Getty Images)

Pages 186–87 – Brown delivers his keynote speech at the 2005 Labour Party Conference. (Courtesy of Getty Images)

Page 196 – Brown officially accepts the nomination to succeed Tony Blair as leader of the Labour Party and Prime Minister on 17 May 2007. (Courtesy of Getty Images)

Page 216 – Gordon Brown with his wife Sarah. (Courtesy of Topfoto)